D1108461

NO LONGER PROPERTY OF
SEATTLE PUBLIC LIBRARY

I am not SPOCK

OTHER BOOKS BY LEONARD NIMOY

You and I

Will I Think of You ?

Leonard Nimoy

I am not SPOCK

Buccaneer Books
Cutchogue, New York

"If I Were a Rich Man" by Sheldon Harnick and Jerry Boch. Copyright © 1964 The New York Times Music Corporation (Sunbeam Division). All rights administered by The New York Times Music Corporation. Used by permission. All rights reserved.

"If We Only Have Love" by Jacques Brel. Copyright © 1968 by Unichappell Music, Inc. All rights reserved. Used by permission of Unichappell Music, Inc.

Copyright © 1975 by Leonard Nimoy

International Standard Book Number: 1-56849-691-5

For ordering information, contact:

Buccaneer Books, Inc.
P.O. Box 168
Cutchogue, N.Y. 11935

(631) 734-5724, Fax (631) 734-7920
www.BuccaneerBooks.com

Contents

The Alien Connection 4

I Am Not Spock 12

Metamorphosis 22

Warp One 32

Impact: The Public and The Press 43

Spock and Me 58

A Family Affair 72

Why? 91

Instant Replays 102

Mission to *Mission* 109

The Goodies Box 118

Live Long and Prosper—L'Chaim 126

Introduction

I don't go around introducing myself to strangers as Mr. Spock. But when someone addresses a letter to "Mr. Spock, Hollywood, California," I'm the one who gets it.

Most people play many roles in their lives. Roles like parent, child, breadwinner, homemaker, brother, sister, friend and lover. But most function under one collective role—individual identity.

Not so in my case. I am identified in at least two specific roles. Leonard Nimoy—actor, and Mr. Spock—Vulcan.

"I didn't recognize you without your pointed ears." I hear that all the time. It's a joke, well intended and good natured, and it's a part of my life.

The obvious intention is to communicate with me. "You are Leonard Nimoy, an actor who plays the role of a pointed-eared Vulcan named Mr. Spock on *Star Trek.*"

Let's try a variation. "You are Mr. Spock of *Star Trek*. You are standing here now, looking like a human named Leonard Nimoy. Therefore, I had difficulty recognizing you."

One more variation. A parent holding a bewildered child by the hand says, "Johnny, this is Mr. Spock. Don't you recognize him?" The child stares and in his eyes I see no recognition. If he had the verbal skills he would probably say, "No. That's not Mr. Spock. Mr. Spock has pointed ears and arched eyebrows and greenish skin and wears his hair in bangs and he has a uniform with a blue shirt and black pants and boots and he's on TV. This man doesn't have any of those things and he's not on TV, he's standing here in front of me!"

Who is correct, the parent or the child?

Star Trek and Nostalgia

There was a time, some of us remember, when the difference between the good guys and the bad guys was quite clear. When we went to war we knew exactly who the enemy was and what he stood for and we believed firmly in the concept that we were right: God was on our side, and the enemy stood for all that was negative and evil and had to be vanquished. Freedom was an easy concept to relate to and the protection of it was all important. True, we sometimes found ourselves with strange bedfellows as allies, but united in common effort, we overlooked political and ideological differences in order to fight the more obvious common enemy.

In recent years there has been a major movement toward nostalgic aspects of the past; the romantic notion that it is possible to separate right from wrong. *Star Trek* falls neatly within the realm of this kind of thinking. Obviously the United Spaceship *Enterprise* is a good thing. Obviously the crew functions as a successful team of good guys intent on doing the "right thing." Obviously the Klingons are bad guys. They have no redeeming qualities and must be dealt with firmly and aggressively. And certainly the *Enterprise* and its crew do that. It's very easy to understand who to root for, certainly at least on the most obvious levels. True, within that construction there are questions of different philosophical positions among various members of the crew and between the crew of the *Enterprise* and certain groups of individuals that we encounter. But for the most part the guys on the *Enterprise* are the guys in the white hats and danger to them represents danger to the viewer. Success for them is success for the viewer.

The nonintervention concept of the Space Federation in retrospect seems like perhaps the most obvious lesson that might well have been studied by our contemporary leadership. The *Enterprise* is on a mission which specifically disallows intervention in the natural evolution of any given society. The concept is to offer aid and assistance without dictating policies or ideologies or lifestyles.

It's all so delightfully simple. It's easy to relate to, fun to watch and it presents no internal conflicts at the identity level. Would that our own society today were as uncomplicated.

Today, seven years after the completion of the last episode, the *Star Trek* series is a legend. I'm very proud of having been connected with the show. I feel that it dealt with morality and philosophical questions in a way that many of us would wish were part of the reality of our lives.

The show has certainly given me a sense of self-worth and particularly the relationship with the character of Mr. Spock has given me a constant guideline for a dignified approach to life as a human being. This book, therefore, is dedicated with deep gratitude to every one of the wonderful individuals who gave so much of their creativity and energy to make the series something special and, of course, to the millions of viewers who took the show into their hearts.

The Alien Connection

I remember sitting in the dark movie house on a Saturday afternoon. On the screen was a great performer in one of the classic roles of all time . . . Charles Laughton, bent over, carrying a grotesque weight, the hump on his back. He was a freak, a horrible mistake of nature hidden away in the bell towers of Notre Dame, the awful, disfigured creature called "Quasimodo," the Hunchback of Notre Dame.

I watched them put him on public display on a wooden turntable in the cathedral courtyard. They whipped him. I don't remember why. Drunk in public or something like that. The crowds laughed at him. Jeered his pain and his humiliation.

Time passed and he rotated on the turntable, bound to it by the ropes. Then thirst set in and he cried out, "Water." The crowd laughed.

Again he cried out for water in that pained distorted speech. The crowd laughed again and someone splashed him with the contents of a slop bucket. And then a beautiful thing happened. The lovely Esmeralda, although terrified by this awful, ugly creature, brought him some water.

And later, when the punishment was finished and Quasimodo's brother took him back into the cathedral, I heard the words. The Hunchback turned his head up toward his brother and with a simple sentence, tore my heart out. "She gave me water." I was glad the theatre was dark so that I could cry freely, and I did.

And then there was another. Boris Karloff. We shivered with fright when the Frankenstein monster came to life. All that awful size and power. Brute dumb force. He'd sneak up quietly behind the heroine and we'd scream to her, "Look out! Turn around, he's behind you." It was terrifying. And then he broke loose. Escaped! Death and terror unshackled. He came across a little girl and we knew that the worst would happen. This brute would kill her! Tear her to pieces. She wasn't afraid. She wasn't wise enough to be afraid! She tried to play with him. And in that instant when we all thought her life had run its course, she offered him a flower . . . and she lived. She had touched something in this monster's being and she lived.

And then, as Spock, I played one of those moments. When in one episode a lady offered me love and completed the connection from Laughton to Karloff to Nimoy. The love connection between human and alien.

There is a moment when we are all touched by the humanity in these creatures that are supposedly inhuman, when the character, Spock, the Frankenstein monster, or Quasimodo, says, "I, too, need love." Millions respond and love pours out because we all need it and we all understand. When one is touched, by a flower or a drink of water, then we are all touched and we can cry for him and for ourselves. Tears of connection. And now I realize that all of this was preparation for the role of Spock. Crying for Quasimodo's heart inside that awful body. Loving the monster who spared the child. Joining with humanity to share understanding and compassion.

These very simple and obviously human experiences were the best preparation an actor could have to play the supposedly ahuman Spock. Spock was not my first experience playing alienated characters.

In 1960, while studying acting with Jeff Corey, I met Vic Morrow. Vic was best known for his work in *Blackboard Jungle*, and would soon star in the *Combat* TV series. He had just recently finished work in a New York production of Jean Genet's *Deathwatch*. Genet's work was available in the underground press, but had never been seen onstage on the West Coast. Eventually, *The Blacks*, *The Maids* and *The Balcony* would be staged. Morrow obtained the West Coast rights to *Deathwatch* and scheduled the first Genet production to be seen there.

In the cast were Michael Forest as the convicted murderer, "Greeneyes," Paul Mazursky, who later produced, wrote and directed such films as *Bob and Carol and Ted and Alice* and *Harry and Tonto*, playing a petty thief named "Maurice," and myself, playing, of course, an alienated intellectual. The three characters are in a prison cell in France. Each is struggling to establish or preserve an identity.

Of the three, Greeneyes and Maurice are what Genet might refer to as "natural" criminals. They are in the criminal life by circumstance and design of fate. My character, "Le-Franc," is there by choice. He has made a conscious effort to join the world of the criminal because he identifies with it. Eventually he is rejected by the prison society in the same way a body would reject an unacceptable kidney. This, in spite of the fact that he commits a murder in a desperate effort to be accepted by his fellow inmates. He finds himself totally alienated from both worlds, the society outside, and the one within the prison walls. In a sense, he has done better than he had hoped for. In trying to alienate himself from one group to join another, he has reached pure alien status, and when he recognizes this fact, he enjoys it.

The production attracted a lot of attention within the movie and TV industry. It brought new impetus to my acting career which had been moving very slowly. It was another case in which an alien character brought me closer to public and industry recognition.

I'll never really understand why I was chosen to play Mr. Spock. In a metaphysical sense, there seemed to be a sort of inevitability involved. It would be easy to assume that Gene Roddenberry had some sort of uncanny instinct for casting the proper actors in the proper role. In spite of all his talents, I think it is fair to say that Gene is not infallible.

There have been many occasions in my acting career when I wanted a particular role desperately. In some cases I have campaigned very hard to get a certain part. Most of these campaigns have failed. Once or twice I have succeeded in convincing a skeptical director or producer. But in the over-whelming majority of cases, casting decisions are made in a rarefied atmosphere which does not leave much room for actors' opinions.

When I was called to meet Gene Roddenberry, I assumed I was to be auditioned. I didn't quite know how to react when I discovered that I was being "sold" on the role.

I was teaching acting classes for five years before the first *Star Trek* pilot was filmed.

In 1960, having been a student in his classes for two years, Jeff Corey asked me to teach for him. I did for two years and then opened my own studio where I taught for three years more.

The approach to the teaching was heavily influenced by the concepts of Stanislavski. In my case, I was particularly committed to the concepts he expressed in *Building a Character*. I am very much affected by the clothes I wear. Putting on a cape can make me feel quite dashing and romantic. An old work jacket, work boots and an old dirty cap can make me feel quite seedy. The character clothes begin to affect me inwardly as does the make-up. There are various other elements which will lead me to the core of the charac-ter. But the externals to me are very helpful.

In 1951, I was cast in the title role of a very modest film called *Kid Monk Baroni*. It was a tremendous break for a 20-year-old kid in Hollywood only a year. The story is about an Italian boy from New York's East Side, born with a disfigured face. He becomes a boxer. Lee Greenway was hired to do the make-up which required foam rubber appliances to accomplish the facial distortions. When he put them on me—the mouth, nose and forehead—I studied myself carefully in the mirror. I was not a thoroughly trained actor, but instinctively my emotions began to respond to my new appearance. I could begin to identify with the internal life of this face—the insecurities, the retiring shyness, the bursts of anger, the paranoia.

I found a home behind that make-up. I was much more confident and comfortable than I would have been had I been told I was to play "a handsome young man."

Even in *Kid Monk Baroni* I was playing a character outside of the social mainstream—separate, unequal and alien. I had been raised in a neighborhood rich in Italian culture. Most of my early friends were Italians. Being Jewish, I always sensed some element of difference, of separation. Our friendships stopped abruptly at the door of the church.

When I was 17, I was cast as "Ralphie," the teenage son of the Berger family in an amateur production of Clifford Odets' *Awake and Sing*. The play deals with a matriarchal Jewish family during the Depression. Ralphie struggles and squirms under the domination of the mother, searching for his identity and finally moving into his own life with the help of some insurance money left by his grandfather. This role, the young man surrounded by a hostile and repressive environment, so touched a responsive chord, that I decided to make a career of acting.

I have played a great variety of roles since. But I still feel most comfortable playing characters that continue the line from "Ralphie" to "Monk Baroni" to "Spock." One of my most gratifying acting experiences in recent years was "Tevye" in *Fiddler on the Roof*. Here again was a man who tried to cope with the dramatic social changes in his society, struggled to hold onto crumbling traditions, and yet was considered alien by the Russian society.

Arthur Miller once wrote, "All plays we call great, let alone those we call serious, are ultimately involved with some aspects of a single problem: It is this—How may a man make of the outside world a home? How and in what ways must he struggle, what must he strive to change and overcome within himself and outside himself if he is to find the safety, the surroundings of love, the ease of soul, the sense of identity and honor, which evidently, all men have connected in their memories with the idea of the family?"

This concept has always excited me, and it is certainly applicable to the characters I have just mentioned. In the broadest sense it applies to Mr. Spock and the *Star Trek* series.

Several major television characters in recent years strike me as being based on the concept of a man out of his element. "Columbo," the scruffy, hardworking detective, often finds himself dealing with adversaries surrounded by wealth, comfort, nobility and social standing. Almost apologetically he pursues the threads of the crime to the ultimate conclusion until, with a touch of embarrassment, he is forced to conclude that his social superior is the murderer.

"McCloud" is the country boy who should be lost in the Big City. But he makes out quite well. The recent "Petrocelli" is functioning in the Southwest against a built-in resentment of his "Eastern lawyer" image.

My early years in Hollywood were heavily influenced by Marlon Brando. The uniform was T-shirt and jeans. The Sunset Strip was very quiet in the early '50s. I worked at an ice cream parlor until 1:00 A.M. and then walked the Strip for several blocks to get to my rooming house. I was stopped regularly by the police. "Where do you live?" "Where are you coming from?" "Do you have any ID?" I got used to it, and eventually they began to recognize me and simply wave as they drove past.

The rooming house was the former residence of Ruth Roman, another Bostonian who had achieved stardom in *The Champion* with Kirk Douglas. When I left the Pasadena Playhouse after six months, I contacted her. She suggested the house because it was cheap and would put me in touch with other young actors and actresses. Several months later she was to play a Spanish lady in a western called *Dallas* with Gary Cooper. The film was to be shot at Warner Brothers. In the script, she had a younger brother who had been educated in Boston. He was a bitter young man who was crippled as the result of a gunshot wound in the leg. She gave me the script. I read it, and felt completely at home with this alienated character. My agent arranged an interview. I met the producer and the director who decided they would give me a screen test in two weeks. A tremendous break! I felt confident of getting the role, but even if I didn't, the test would be valuable, because I would be "on film" which could be borrowed and shown at other studios.

Two weeks later, to the day, I was called and told to report to Warners "immediately." I was confused. If I were to be tested I would have had more advance notice. When I arrived, I discovered that work was already in progress and the film was being shot. My character was to start filming the very next day on location. I was to have only a reading. I did it and was sent home.

The next day my agent was informed that the part had been cast with another actor and the company was away on location. The producer, who was in his office on the lot, wouldn't accept a call from my agent or me. I got on a bus and went to the studio, slipped past the guards and up to his office. His secretary phoned in to announce me. He said he was busy. I told her, "I'll wait," and sat down to sweat it out.

I think I'd seen it done that way by John Garfield in the movies of the '40s. About half an hour went by. The secretary was nervous and embarrassed. She tried again, "Mr. Nimoy is still out here waiting." And then I heard the voice over the phone and through the connecting door. "Tell him to get the

hell out of here or I'll call the studio police!" "Yes, sir," she
said quietly and hung up the phone. "Did you hear him?" she
asked. She seemed sympathetic, but she was being forced
into the middle of a bad situation and the look on her face
said, "He'll do it, too." I said, "Yes, I heard him . . ." and left.

The next day, the front page of *Variety* carried a story
about producers and directors on the Warners lot complaining
that actors and agents were arriving without appointments
and interrupting the work. Security measures would be taken
to prevent further incidents of this kind.

It was all perfect. Having been refused the role of the alien
in his movie, I played it out in his office, and then was
banished from his planet!

I have heard stories told about actors who would "break
into Hollywood" by renting a Rolls Royce and spending their
time meeting industry people at poolside at the Beverly Hills
Hotel. My approach was quite the opposite. It was the jeans
and dirty old car routine. "I'm an artist. If you want me, you
have to accept me on my own terms and in spite of my
differences." Sounds like Mr. Spock, doesn't it? In Spock I
finally found the best of both worlds: to be widely accepted in
public approval and yet be able to continue to play the
insulated alien through the Vulcan character.

I Am Not Spock

I am not Spock.

Then why does my head turn in response to a stranger on the street who calls out that name? Why do I feel a twinge when someone says, "What happened to your ears?" I am not Spock.

Then why do I feel a wonderful warmth when I hear or read a compliment aimed at the Vulcan?

Spock for President reads the bumper sticker on the car in front of me. I'm filled with pride and I smile. I'm not Spock.

But if I'm not, who is? And if I'm not Spock, then who am I?

I have a brother, Melvin. He lives 3,000 miles away. We have a good relationship. But it's different. Yes, if someone compliments him, I take pride. If someone were to malign him, I would be hurt. But he is he. I am not him and he is not me. We exist independently. Spock and I do not. So, Spock is not my brother.

What is this relationship between Spock and me? Is it like the Corsican brothers? Even when miles apart one felt the pain when the other was injured! Empathy. Maybe that's the answer. But there's a difference. The Corsican brothers could exist in two different places at the same time. Spock and I cannot.

And it's more complicated than that. Perhaps worse than that. The question is, without Spock, who am I? Do I, or would I, exist at all without him? And without me, who is he? I suspect he might do better without me than I without him. That bothers me. Or more accurately, it concerns me.

That's why I'm writing this book. Maybe if I can get it all down on paper and see the words and ideas staring me in the face I might understand. I might get a better fix on what I am and who he is. With Spock and me it's a unique game of "I'm O.K. We're O.K."

I might get to know something about myself that millions of others know better than I. If I could only see myself as others see me.

Recently I sat with a group of actors I'd just met. We talked of theatre, plays, TV, characters. Good talk. And then as I was leaving one of the actresses said, "Leonard, we love you." I smiled and I was warmed. I said, "Thank you" but I wanted to add, "I'll tell him when I see him."

She loves Spock! I know it! I'm sure of it! But to whom else could she say those words? They must be said to me, or more precisely, through me. Yes, there was a sense of camaraderie. Actors talking to actors. Creators of characters talking to one of their own who has created a character who has become legendary.

That's nice. More than nice, it's wonderful. But standing silently behind my shoulder is a very jealous, ever-present Vulcan!!

SPOCK: Tell her I accept her compliment, emotional though
  it may be.

NIMOY: What compliment?

SPOCK: She said they love me.

NIMOY: That is not what she said. She specifically said,
  "Leonard, we love you." And I know there's nothing
  wrong with your hearing!

SPOCK: If you're so certain of her intent, why are you becoming agitated?

NIMOY: That's ridiculous. Every time I'm paid a compliment
  you grab it away. You grab it up for yourself!

SPOCK: Would she have paid you that compliment if not for
  me?

NIMOY: No!

SPOCK: Then how can you claim it for your own?

You see what I mean?

    I walked onstage in a performance of *Caligula* night after
night, convinced that I was Leonard Nimoy giving a good
performance as the mad emperor. "We are resolved to be
logical." That was one of my lines. And night after night I
dreaded it. I dreaded the moment when that word would fall
out of my mouth. "Logical"—that's *his* word. Spock's word,
and everybody knows it. But I had to say it. I wanted to
swallow it, mumble it, chew it up, rather than say it! Why?
Because I knew that the moment those three syllables
sounded through the theatre, *he* would be there! That alien
would be there, demanding what was his! Identity.

    I struggled with it. Night after night. I approached it like a
horse approaching a fence, not wanting to jump but knowing
that I must. Searching for an escape, dreading the moment
when I could hear or almost hear that laugh which would
follow the utterance. That communal laugh of recognition
which would say, "He's here. Spock is here."

SPOCK: Greetings—you've been away.

NIMOY: Yes, doing a play in Austin, Texas.

SPOCK: And the title?

NIMOY: *Caligula*.

SPOCK: Oh yes—the Roman emperor.

NIMOY (surprised): That's right! You know his story?

SPOCK: He was quite mad. . . .

NIMOY: They say he was a good man until he became mentally disturbed.

SPOCK: Yes, I remember also that one theory ascribed his madness to a love potion given him by his mistress.

NIMOY: Right!

SPOCK: Who authored the play?

NIMOY: Albert Camus. When he was only 25.

SPOCK: Oh yes . . . The French existentialist. A contemporary of Sartre and Gide . . .

NIMOY: Spock, you amaze me.

SPOCK: Of course . . . and what is his theme?

NIMOY: "Men die, and they are not happy."

SPOCK: Ah. . . . the pursuit of happiness does frequently have tragic consequences.

NIMOY: Let me put it another way. Caligula, in his madness wants "to change the scheme of things" . . . to teach his people to demand more of themselves and each other.

SPOCK: And how does he proceed. . . .?

NIMOY (hesitantly): By insisting that they take action based on logic rather than emotion.

SPOCK: Brilliant! I must reread my Camus.

NIMOY (springing the trap): But Caligula is mad . . . and even he, in the end, realizes he's lost his way.

SPOCK: Unfortunate. A fine idea gone astray in the hands of an unbalanced human.

NIMOY: Spock . . . this competition between us is silly . . .

SPOCK: I'm not aware that one exists . . .

NIMOY: Well, it does . . . and it's silly . . . don't forget that
   I'm real and you're only a fictitious character.

SPOCK: Are you sure?

I am not Spock.

But I'm close to him. Closer than anyone. How much closer can two people be than to stand in the same body, occupy the same space?

Yes, there are benefits. I have an audience, a platform because of him. But it must be shared. I have written two books of poetry. They have been widely circulated and well-received. The one word which comes back most consistently is "surprising."

Why surprising? "Because," I'm told, "the writing is *sensitive.*" "Thank you, but why should that be surprising?" "Because one doesn't expect sensitive poetry from a cool, rational, pragmatic, logical person." "But you're talking about Spock! I'm not Spock!" "Oh really?"

I like being Spock. But I like myself too. I'd like to be me independent of him. I try—very hard, but it's tough. Sometimes I think I've done it. Sometimes I work very hard at doing my things, thinking my thoughts. To be me, Leonard Nimoy. Sometimes I think I've got it made! Then I'll get on an airplane and somebody'll flash me a Vulcan salute. Or some nice lady will ask for my autograph and I'll proudly sign, "Leonard Nimoy," and then she'll say, "Please sign *Mr. Spock.* That's the way my son knows you."

So sometimes I get tired of the struggle and I simply sign, *Spock.* I tell myself it's faster. It's only five letters instead of twelve. But who am I kidding? No one. I do it because the look in this particular child's eyes says, "I love you, Mr. Spock" and I know that if I signed any other name, two people would be cheated: The child and Spock, and I can't do that. I don't want to hurt that child, and I must be fair to the Vulcan. I think he would do the same for me.

I am not Spock.

But given the choice, if I had to be someone else, I would be Spock. If someone said, "You can have the choice of being any other TV character ever played," I would choose Spock. I like him. I admire him. I respect him.

If someone could wave a magic wand and make him go away, disappear forever, I wouldn't let them do it. I would choose to keep him alive. I don't really have that choice. He'll be around anyway. But if I had that choice I would keep him alive. He stands for something that makes me feel good. Dignity and honesty and a lot more. And whatever of that rubs off on me makes me feel good.

But, I am not Spock.

I have a daughter, Julie, born March 21, 1955, 9:30 P.M. EST—Atlanta, Georgia.

I have a son, Adam, born August 9, 1956, 11:22 P.M. PST—Los Angeles, California.

Two miracles. And yet not miraculous. Miraculous to me suggests unusual. These two events are unusual to me because they happened only those two times in my life, but thousands of these events take place on our planet everyday. We call them "miracles" and then we go about our business.

When Julie was born I was in the next room. I heard the sounds of labor; I heard the silence of relief from pain. I heard the first cries and I looked at my watch.

When Adam was born I was three thousand miles away working in upstate New York on a TV episode. The phone rang. My father-in-law said, "You've got a son!" and gave me the positive health report on mother and child and I looked at my watch.

In the physical and spiritual sense, I was involved in another birth, that of the alien, Mr. Spock. I was present. More present in some ways than in the two cases I've just described. I suffered the labor pains, but I don't think I'm the mother.

There were no doctors in attendance. It was not a medical procedure. There were no first cries and there was no precise recording of the time. I didn't look at my watch.

It's frustrating. I don't know exactly when it happened. I recall vividly when the seed of this life was planted. I can still see the face of Gene Roddenberry, the man who did the planting. I can recall his voice and his words but, the birth, I don't know exactly when it took place and it's frustrating.

I have given birth to, or been present at the birth of, other characters. In some cases I can recall the instant that the new life arrived. In some, I can't, but that doesn't bother me. In this case it does. It's important somehow.

This being, this particular being, is still here in a very real sense. Still with me and, through me, with millions of others. He still affects my life and that of many others. Living because of me, going where I go, doing what I do. Affecting my speech, my walk, my thinking, my life.

My children, Adam and Julie, are grown. They are "away at school." But this alien, although grown, is never "away." I suspect that if I knew exactly when he began, I could have a more definite feeling about when we would end. If, in fact, I were to desire that end.

I wanted this birth. In a physical sense, I worked harder for this one than I did for the others. But somewhere I lost control. This being, this character, this "life" sneaked up on me. Not in one tidy, precise moment, but in a mosaic of tiny events, in several mini-births, over a period of at least a year and a half. From the first seed-planting conversation with Gene Roddenberry through weeks of thought and gestation. Through countless hours in front of mirrors. Through eternities of tedious sessions with tailors. Through turbulent nights of tossing, turning in my brain, dredging up bits and pieces of ideas, trying them in the puzzle pattern, keeping some and discarding others.

There was even a premature semi-birth in what was called, "the first *Star Trek* pilot." And then back into incubation for a year or more. There was even a semi-death when NBC rejected that first pilot and particularly the character. "Wrong," they said, "this must not live. This strange alien life is not to be." They had no idea how stubborn this entity could and would be. How determined to live!

They were successful in putting to death all the other characters in the world called *Star Trek.* Easily. There was no outcry. There was no criminal investigation—no inquiry. They simply placed an order for production of a second pilot and a new group was born. Captain Kirk, Dr. McCoy, Scotty, Sulu, Uhura and so on, full-blown from the brow of Zeus. But this one, the character named Spock, refused to die. He simply watched, perhaps smiling internally and waiting patiently. Then he stepped into his place in this recreated, reordered, repopulated society and he lived. And he lives. Oh how he lives.

I suppose I could be arbitrary about it and establish an artifical date of birth. Thursday, September 8, 1966, 7:30 P.M. EST. The first televised appearance of *Star Trek* and Mr. Spock. But somehow that doesn't satisfy me. The character was born before this. In this book I will mention several incidents which took place during the development of the character before that September date, any one of these would make a more appropriate "birthdate." And perhaps that's the answer. Perhaps Spock had many births. It's possible that various aspects of the character were born at different times. Still I search for a key moment.

In May of 1975 I was rehearsing at one of the Drury Lane theatres in Chicago for a production of *The Fourposter,* a two-character play spanning some 40 years. My partner, Ann Eggert, and I had a terrible creative struggle in our efforts to master the first scene—the young teenage couple arriving in their bedroom on their wedding night. It is a delightful scene. Later it was to be a joy to play. But she and I both had to shed years of maturity, wisdom and experience to capture the simplicity of those two people at that time in their lives.

Day after day in rehearsals it was wrong. So wrong it was painful. But then on the 8th day of rehearsal it happened. I looked at her and she was my bride, young, silly, charming and beautiful. And she must have seen her young groom. Awkward, excited and embarrassed. The characters were born and the scene came to life. And when we were finished, and I knew that it was right, I was terribly depressed. I suddenly realized that I had had a glimpse back into the innocence of my own youth.

There was a very profound feeling of loss; it was romantic, not real. Because, in truth, that was a very painful period in my life as it is for most of us. But I had touched that universal "loss of innocence" that the poets talk about. The artist in me felt a sense of relief because I now had a grip on the character. But the human me felt something quite different.

It was a moment and an experience that I will always remember whenever I think of "Michael" in *The Fourposter*.

In the case of Spock, time passes and I doubt that I will ever have that one profound moment to look back on and say, "That's when he was born."

And what about me? Why me? Why am I connected with an indestructible umbilical cord to this creature? What sensible connection? What clues in my lineage, my parentage, my childhood, my environment would suggest this connection? What preparation, what reading, thinking, fantasizing, would lead a researcher to say, "Aha! That's how it began. That's why he was chosen!" None. Absolutely none.

If the lists of all the members of the Screen Actors Guild had been tacked to a wall, and Gene Roddenberry had thrown a dart and assigned the role to the actor whose name was struck by the point, the choice could easily have made as much sense at least in "logical" terms. But I hardly dare use that word. That word *logic* belongs to him, this alien, this force, this child, father, brother of mine—Spock.

Let's turn to magic. Maybe that's where the answer lies. I've been told as much. Told that I was "chosen" in a metaphysical sense. That I am a channel—a vessel. Chosen by nonearthly means by nonhuman beings to house this "life." Maybe so. It makes as much sense as the other more "real" possibilities!

Let's try lineage. Descended from Russian, nonartist, extremely pragmatic earthly parents. Father—a barber. Nothing there to hold onto as a clue. Except perhaps that my parents came here, to the United States, as aliens. Maybe that's important.

I'm a college dropout. Does that help? Maybe. The key word is *out*. I must admit that could be useful. In high school my favorite subjects were English and physics. I almost hate to admit it because Spock certainly has a command of both!

Something makes me want to deny it. To deny that there's any sense to the whole thing and yet there may be some pattern after all—some real connection. Some preparation for this possession.

For that's what it was. A possession. Not without rewards. There have been many. And, scanning the events from the seeding through the labor pains to the present, one event rings clear as a special moment. Perhaps it should be called "the end of the beginning." April 1967. No doctors or nurses in attendance. Only our mailman. He dropped a letter in our slot. It hit the floor in our living room. The return address was the Academy of TV Arts and Sciences.

> Dear Mr. Nimoy:
>
> It gives us great pleasure to inform you that you have been nominated for an Emmy in the category: Best performance by an actor in a continuing supporting role in a TV series.

My wife and I embraced each other and cried.
Maybe I should have looked at my watch!

Metamorphosis

For three years, twelve hours a day, five days a week, approximately ten months of each year, I functioned as an extraterrestrial.

Many people have had some experience with role playing. Some people have had more experience than I; some people have played a particular role longer than I. But given my intense commitment to the identification with this role, and given the unique nature of this extraterrestrial, there may be some value in reassembling the experience.

Six years after having completed the role, I am still affected by the character of Spock, the Vulcan First Officer and Science Officer of the Starship *Enterprise*. Of course, the role changed my career. Or rather, gave me one. It made me wealthy by most standards and opened up vast opportunities. It also affected me very deeply and personally, socially, psychologically, emotionally. To this day I sense Vulcan speech patterns, Vulcan social attitudes and even Vulcan patterns of logic and emotional suppression in my behavior.

What started out as a welcome job to a hungry actor, has become a constant and ongoing influence in my thinking and lifestyle.

In 1965, Gene Roddenberry was producing a TV series for NBC titled *The Lieutenant*. It starred Gary Lockwood and had to do with his adventures as a Marine Corps officer. My agent at that time, Alex Brewis, had submitted me for a guest starring role.

The feeling of the director and the casting people, was that I was not suitable for the role. The character was a very garrulous individual who was a Hollywood motion picture star wanting to make a movie about the Marine Corps.

Prior to that time, the major roles that I had had were rather internal whereas this one called for a very outgoing externalized performance. To my agent's credit, he persisted and Marc Daniels, the director of the episode, agreed to interview me and let me read a scene for him. In a very brief meeting which lasted no longer than ten minutes I read for Marc, and he agreed that I could do the role, and I was hired. That same director, Marc Daniels, was to become a very good friend and a director of a large number of our *Star Trek* episodes.

When the episode was finished, Gene Roddenberry commented to my agent that he was writing a script for a science fiction TV series and he had a role that he wanted me to play. My agent reported this to me but I didn't pay much attention, assuming it would be some time before the script reached the production stage and it was silly to raise my hopes.

However, several months later Gene did call and a meeting was arranged. At that first meeting it was my assumption that I was being interviewed for the role. Gene's conversation threw me off balance because he seemed to be selling me on the idea of working in his series. He took the trouble to walk me through the prop department and the scenic design shop to show me the nature of the work that was being done for the series. Above all he seemed to be trying to impress upon me the fact that this series was being very carefully prepared and that it would be indeed something special to television.

I was so excited at the prospect of getting a steady job on a television series that I tried very hard to keep my mouth shut. I felt that the more I talked the more chance there was of talking myself out of what could be steady work. I left Gene's office very excited and expected negotiations to begin. Several days passed during which I wondered if perhaps I had said something wrong in my meeting with Gene. Then the phone call came and my agent informed me that we had run into a slight catch. Gene wanted to see some film of other performances that I had done "in order to know how to best write the role for me."

This sounded like a very nice way of checking further into my acting capabilities to determine whether or not in fact I was to be given the role.

We agreed to show a film which was a performance that I had done on a *Dr. Kildare* episode, a couple of years previous. This particular film was chosen because it was quite the opposite of the boisterous character that I had played on *The Lieutenant* show. Gene saw the film and then negotiations did indeed move ahead. He later told me that he was extremely impressed with the Kildare performance and that he had actually seen it when it was first televised. He flattered me by telling me that he was not aware that the actor in that case and the actor in his show were one and the same. The range of performance was so different.

So in fact the die was cast and I was to become Mr. Spock, son of Sarek, the Vulcan, and Amanda, the Earth scientist, in the science fiction adventure series called *Star Trek*.

Roddenberry and I had numerous meetings to discuss the nature of the character and his background. The Vulcans had been a violent and emotional people, which almost led to their destruction. They made a decision. Thenceforth emotion was to be foreign to the Vulcan nature. Logic would rule. Vulcans would be distinguished in appearance by their skin color, hair style and pointed ears, a race concerned with dignity and progress, incorporating the culture and ritual of the past with the best of what the future could offer. In Spock there would be a special mixture of tensions. The logic and emotional suppression of the Vulcan people through the father, Sarek, pitted against the emotional and humanistic traits inherited from the human mother, Amanda.

These were rich beginnings for a TV character and especially challenging for an actor whose idols were Lon Chaney and Paul Muni, both great character actors of the past, but I had mixed feelings about it. At this point my career wasn't exactly what one would call extraordinary, but I was making a living as an actor and as a teacher. Most important, I took a great pride in my reputation as a solid character actor. I had reached the point where I was able to be somewhat selective about the roles I played, accepting only those which I thought had merit and offered opportunities to play dimensional people. As yet, I had not read a *Star Trek* script. I was very much concerned about the possibility of getting involved in what might turn out to be a "mickey mouse" character. I felt it could be a ludicrous adventure, possibly leading to embarrassment for myself and the other people involved.

I discussed the problems with Vic Morrow, an actor whose talent and judgment I respected. Vic and I went through the pros and cons of the situation and even at one point touched on the possibility of devising a make-up that would be so complete that Leonard Nimoy would be totally unrecognizable. In this way I could do the job, earn the money and avoid the dangers of being connected with a ludicrous character.

Of course, it didn't work out that way and I am very happy with the way the matter resolved itself. But, to this day, I still think it might have been fun to have played that character totally hidden and be totally mysterious and unavailable in my private life. It could have been the put-on of the century. Just imagine the headlines in the newspapers and magazines:

ACTUAL ALIEN AGREES TO APPEAR IN SCIENCE FICTION TV SERIES.

In any case, I finally decided to plunge in and make a commitment. Gene Roddenberry and I shook hands on our deal with mutual good faith and excitement. We were giving birth to an extraterrestrial.

The first physical labor pains took place in a make-up room at the Desilu Studios in Hollywood. I sat down in front of a mirror, and Lee Greenway, a durable make-up man and old acquaintance from *Kid Monk Baroni,* started to experiment with an admittedly crude application of the first pair of pointed ears. They were "built-up" with layers of paper tissue and liquid latex, never expected to be acceptable but only to give an indication of what the effect might be. Well, it was as bizarre as the result of a child playing with her mother's make-up. It was gruesome, ludicrous and very depressing. Roddenberry and Herb Solow, head of television production at the studio, asked my permission to run some video tape on me, to be studied in the projection room. I agreed and was led onto the stage of *I Love Lucy.* Fortunately the audience had not arrived for the day's taping. But the crew, 15 or 20 craftsmen, was asked to light me and run some footage.

The results were painful. Had the make-up been complete, the wardrobe present, the character fully realized, it would have been difficult. Under the circumstances, dressed in very casual street clothes with a crude pair of pointed ears, in the context of the *I Love Lucy* set, it was, to say the least, painful. And yet, here it was, the beginning of the public exposure of the extraterrestrial.

I found myself taking mental notes. Storing away emotional memories which might someday be useful in the role. Those feelings of being alien, almost to the point of being ridiculous. Knowing that each of these people would be composing clever lines of dialogue to exchange after I had gone. These were the real seeds from which the emotional structure of Spock would grow.

I was moving into the world of an extraterrestrial. Already I could feel myself building defenses, attempting to elevate my thinking above and beyond a concern for the opinion of *mere humans.* I was of another realm and they could think what they would.

Several weeks later, I would have a similar experience during the first day of shooting on the pilot film. Fully wardrobed in the uniform prescribed by Starfleet, and in full make-up, I stepped onto the sound stage at the studio for the first time. This time, at least in a physical sense, the character was complete.

My agent was there to greet me. With him was a lovely female client. Her reaction was startling. She was open and obvious in her interest, and gave me my first exposure to the generous and gratifying female reaction which was to come, synthesized in Dr. Isaac Asimov's later description of Spock as "a security blanket with sexual overtones."

I should pause at this point and give some credit where it is due. Between the time that Lee Greenway first applied that crude pair of ears and the time we were ready to actually start shooting the pilot, we walked some dangerous paths. Making a proper appliance like a pair of ears that is believable is a very sophisticated and special task. The studio, Desilu at that time, had contracted with a special effects company who were to design and build most of the special gear for creatures on various planets, such as the strange and grotesque heads and foam latex suits and so forth—the type of thing that was seen in the show called "Arena" where Bill Shatner fought a creature called a Gorn. They were asked, among other things, to prepare my ears for the pilot.

There is a vast difference between the type of work they were to do, which would completely cover a man's head or body, and the very delicate appliance work that was necessary for the ears. They went through the necessary procedures much as any make-up or appliance artist would do. A plaster cast was made of the particular feature, in this case my own ears, then a "positive" reproduction was made by pouring a hardening solution into that cast, so that when it was removed they had, in effect, a perfect replica of my own ears. Then an

artist built up the tips of the top edge of the ear with putty
which became, in effect, the "appliance," which eventually
was used. This putty tip then was cast in plaster to make a
mold. Eventually foam rubber of a very delicate nature was
poured into that mold and what emerged was a pair of foam
rubber tips to be applied to my ears.

The first pair was delivered to the studio and Fred Phillips, who was in charge of the make-up department for the
series, applied them and they looked pretty bad. We showed
them to Gene Roddenberry and others involved, and they too
agreed that another effort should be made. This same company then proceeded to try again on two or three occasions
and the results were simply not right. Fred explained to me
that these people were not specialists in this particular field.
The problem was that the studio, having contracted with
them to do all of the special effect work in this area, wanted
these people to deliver the appliances. To go to another
source would mean an additional cost which the studio was
anxious to avoid.

Time was running out. Within a few days we would begin
to shoot the series, and the ears were simply not right. It was
at this point that I went to Gene Roddenberry and told him
that we had a serious problem. The eyebrows, by this time,
were taking shape, the haircut was evolving, the skin tone had
been arrived at, and I felt that perhaps we had best avoid the
ears since we were running into so much trouble.

It's somewhat legendary now that Gene did in fact insist
that we should continue to try to solve the "ear problem." In
this conversation he told me that he felt that it was vital to
maintain one's own original ideas rather than see them
washed away in compromise because of temporary difficul-
ties. He also promised me that we would do thirteen episodes
with these ears and that if I wasn't happy he would write a
script where Mr. Spock got an "ear job."

About three days before the pilot was to be shot, Fred
Phillips had reached the point of desperation. He took it upon
himself without consulting the studio to take me to the lab of a

specialist in delicate appliance work. The procedure started all over again. The plaster cast, the mold, the designing of the tips, the casting, etc., and within about thirty-six hours a pair of ears arrived which were to Fred's satisfaction. These then were the ears which were first used for the original *Star Trek* pilot. To this day, I am most grateful to Fred Phillips for knowing the difference between what was wrong and what was right and having the guts to do something about it. Had he not made that decision the Spock character could have been a comic disaster from the start.

So it began. I went to work and played the scenes. Said the lines. Groping and learning to walk, talk, function as an alien. Putting out the sounds and motions and watching, recording the feedback of my fellow actors, crew personnel and visitors. It was difficult for a long time. The total understanding of the character would only be found in the total context. This rigid pointed-eared creature was only a visual gimmick until perceived as a part of a whole: the particular story we were filming, the ship, the crew, the antagonists, the entire buildup of another world, another time. Taken alone, in bits and pieces, out of context, it was still dangerously close to a joke.

Nevertheless, I began to feel more comfortable. I could understand my place, my function in the stories, my relationship to the other characters. A sense of dignity began to evolve. I took a pride in being different and unique.

Above all, I began to study human behavior from an alien point of view. I began to enjoy the Vulcan position. "These humans are interesting, at times a sad lot, at times foolish, but interesting and worthy of study."

The scripts, particularly the character of Dr. McCoy, the humanist, offered opportunities to deal with the human need to see everything and others only in relation to themselves. "Anybody who isn't like us is strange. Anybody who doesn't want to be like us is a fool."

I was becoming alienated, and didn't realize it. My attitude toward the humans around me became quite paternal.

In some respects I assumed the position of teacher, or role model. My hope was that we could reduce inefficiency and silly emotionalism if I set examples through my higher standards of discipline and precision.

"Nature abhors a vacuum." I showed little or no emotional response, so my co-workers and associates projected responses for me. For example, this quote from a co-worker passed along to me by a friend at the studio: "I see (in Nimoy) a growing image of a shrewd, ambition-dominated man, probing, waiting *with emotions and feelings masked,* ready to leap at the right moment and send others broken and reeling. . . ."

At the onset, the actor felt protective of the character, much as a parent tries to protect a developing child. Certainly my ego was involved and was bruised. But it seemed important to help the character to come to life. When he did, he protected the actor. He became an ever-present friend who could be called upon as an ally in adverse circumstances. Nimoy could submerge himself and let the formidable Spock take over.

Eventually, the show went on the air (September 8, 1966). The reaction was immediate and multiplied at an astounding rate. The magic of Spock became quickly apparent. I was mobbed at personal appearances and security measures were necessary to get me into and out of crowded situations. *Security* and *privacy* suddenly became important words to me and to my family. The mail and phone calls and in general the intense activity that I suddenly experienced made it obvious that we were involved in something that was "happening." Before too long even NBC became actively involved in the "Spock phenomenon."

I discovered later through Gene Roddenberry and Herb Solow that NBC had been very negative about the character and in fact wanted the character removed from the series before the shooting started. Where they had originally felt that "no one would want to identify with the Spock character," they now decided that everyone was identifying. Therefore, they wanted Spock much more actively involved in the stories that would be shot in the future.

Since the whole thing started I had felt a wide range of emotional reaction to my identification with Spock. The range has included at various times a total embracing of the character and a total rejection of the character.

Spock was quickly becoming a pop culture hero. I didn't set out to be a pop culture hero. The simple truth is that I set out to be a craftsmanlike actor, a professional and possibly some day even an artist.

Warp One

The first time I ever saw myself in a movie I was in a state of shock for weeks. I don't really know what I expected, but I couldn't deal with what I saw. That strange skinny figure walking and talking up there on the screen set me squirming in my seat. I appeared in two or three brief scenes, and when each of them began I went into such a state of tension that I was totally unable to relate to what that person on the screen was doing. Had someone told me I was wonderful (they didn't), I would have had to believe it. If they had told me I was awful (mercifully they didn't do that either), I would have been forced to believe that as well. I simply did not "see" or experience myself, and therefore had no basis for judgment.

Years later, having watched that same person on film scores of times, I was able to relax enough to pass objective judgment on my work. Some actors claim they never watch themselves. I had to. I was too curious.

Today, I trust my own taste. I've played enough roles and have seen myself enough times that I can project my performance from the time I first read the script.

I suspect that it's similar to what happens when a block of marble arrives at a sculptor's studio. When he first looks at it, sees the image inside the block and then starts to chip away to reveal it to the eyes of others, the ability to see it is his visionary talent. The ability to chip away the excess is his craft or technique.

When I first sit down to read a script, a performance begins to grow on a screen or stage in my head. If I like that performance, if I am moved to laughter and tears, an audience will have the same experience. If it doesn't play well in my head, something is wrong. Perhaps it's simply not a good script. Perhaps I'm having difficulty relating to or understanding the character. If I can't resolve that difficulty, the chances for a successful performance are very slim. Possibly, with enough rehearsal time, some research, and the help of a good director, the problem can be overcome. But it's an uphill battle.

On the other hand, if I am moved when I read it, and I am still moved when I play it, I will be moved when I see it on the screen. I've seen enough of myself to be able to relax, sit back and be a member of the audience at my own performance.

How do you do it?

Spencer Tracy, when asked for advice on acting said, "Know your lines and don't bump into the furniture." James Cagney said, "Walk in, plant your feet, look the other fellow in the eye . . . and tell the truth." With all due respect to both of these giant talents, I would have to say there's something more.

The true creation of a being, a character other than one's self, for me is comparable to a mystical or spiritual experience. To stand in another person's shoes. To see as he sees, to hear as he hears. To know what he knows, and to do all this with a sense of control, a mastering of the dramatic moment, there must be more than a "natural talent" at work.

In Mexico and Spain, during a bull fight, an ambitious youngster will sometimes leap from the stands into the arena to take on the bull. Very often he makes a fool of himself and possibly is seriously injured as well. If he performs well and captures the imagination of the crowd, instead of being arrested by the police, he may be picked up by an impresario who recognizes his talent and will give him a start in a professional career.

If he does well, chances are he has been practicing somewhere. Possibly he's been sneaking into breeding farms at night to secretly work the bulls until one day he feels ready to make his bid in public.

For many years, Hollywood publicity men sold the public on the idea that stars are found at bus stops and soda fountains. It was very good publicity. It led every young male and female to fantasize about the possibility of being "discovered." That was good for the box office. But it made a mockery of acting as an art.

Tracy and Cagney were able to give very simple answers to the "how do you do it" question. That simplicity was beautifully visible in their work. Behind the simplicity were years of effort, study, trial and failure until all the rubbish that most actors start with was stripped away and only the clarity of finely polished work remained.

Of course, there's "luck" involved in any career. Many very fine and well prepared actors never get the opportunity to achieve wide recognition. It usually comes when the proper role in the proper vehicle finds the right performer.

Many brilliant performances go unnoticed in plays, films or TV shows which do not capture public or industry attention.

In the vast majority of cases, the actor, like most artists, must work for the satisfaction of knowing that his or her work has improved with the passage of time. This knowledge won't pay the rent, but it does help feed the soul.

In my case I had reached the point in my career where I could support my family on my income as an actor and an

acting teacher. Still there was much frustration. I felt I was
not working frequently enough, or in roles challenging
enough to make full use of my craft. I was very seriously
working at starting a career as a director when I was cast in the
role of Mr. Spock. Since *Star Trek* the situation has been
reversed. I've had no time to pursue a directing career.

I did direct one episode of *Night Gallery* in 1972. Jack
Laird, the producer who gave me my virgin assignment on
the show, offered me another one. I had to turn it down
because it conflicted with an appearance in Milwaukee as
"Fagin" in *Oliver*. *Night Gallery* was then cancelled, and that
was that.

Someday, I'll get to it. But for now the challenges are
plentiful in other areas.

In a successful mating of role and actor, there comes a
day—either in rehearsal if it's a play, or during shooting of a
film or TV series—when the character takes hold. The actor
and his technique disappear and the magical transformation
takes place.

During rehearsals of *Death of a Salesman* it happened to
Lee J. Cobb who became "Willy Loman." Arthur Miller,
who, as the playwright, had been watching the rehearsals,
later said, "On that day, a man cast a shadow that was not his
own."

How does that happen? It is a combination of talents.
Writing, directing, and acting. But even with those elements
present there is no guarantee that the magic will take place. It
is not a science, it is an art.

The artists bring together a group of choices, based on
experience and talent. Hopefully this combination of choices
will blend to create the desired effect. When it really "cooks"
the result is greater than the sum of all the parts.

In my case with Spock, there were many choices to be
made, aside from the internal life of the character and the
make-up and costumes. For example, how would he talk?
How would he walk or sit? Did he keep his arms at his side,
did he fold them or clasp his hands behind his back?

In some of these choices I was influenced by a performance given by Harry Belafonte at the Greek Theatre in Los Angeles in the mid-'50s. The Greek Theatre is an amphitheatre which seats several thousand people. Belafonte was at the height of his popularity and the place was packed. From where my wife and I were seated Belafonte was a small, distant figure.

During the first forty-five minutes of his program he stood perfectly still at a center stage microphone, his shoulders slightly hunched, his hands resting on the front of his thighs. He simply sang. Then in the middle of a phrase, he finally made a move. He simply raised his right arm slowly until it was parallel to the floor. For me the impact was enormous. Had he been moving constantly, the gesture would have meant nothing. But following that long period of containment it was as though a cannon had been fired.

I found this idea very useful in Spock. When a stone face lifts an eyebrow, something has happened. The effect is magnifying/magnified. Bit by bit, choice by choice, the character was put together until life was created. Until an actor "cast a shadow that was not his own." When that happens, when the actor sees the people and events around him through the senses of the character, the creative choices work easier.

When it happened to me as Spock, I knew it. I could reject a suggested piece of business with, "A Vulcan wouldn't do that." That's why the Spock neck pinch came into the series.

This was a device which was later mistakenly referred to as the Vulcan death grip. (There is no Vulcan death grip.) The Spock pinch first appeared in an episode called "The Enemy Within" which I shall refer to in more detail later. The scene in which it was introduced was one where Captain Kirk was jeopardized by a character who represented the negative side of his personality. This character was about to destroy Kirk with a phaser. The script called for me to sneak up behind the negative character and hit him over the head with the butt of my phaser.

I was jarred when I read the scene. Something about the action seemed to be totally out of context. I felt that coming up from behind and hitting people on the head with the butt of a gun belonged in the westerns of the 1890s, something one would expect to find in *Gunsmoke* or *Bonanza*. I mentioned this to the director who was willing to go along with the thought and asked what I would suggest as a replacement. I told him that since we were in the 22nd century and that Vulcans were a product of our own creation, we could take the license to devise whatever seemed to fit the situation properly. I suggested that Vulcans had made a thorough study of the human anatomy and that Vulcans were capable of transmitting a special energy from their fingertips which if applied to the proper nerve centers on a human's neck and shoulder, would render a human unconscious. He asked for a demonstration. I explained to Bill Shatner what I had in mind and when I applied the pressure at the proper point, Bill stiffened and dropped in a heap. That's how the Vulcan neck pinch was born.

I am constantly asked how I managed "to keep a straight face" while playing the character. In terms of actor's craft it was easy. I'm always amazed at the speed and deftness with which a plumber fixes a leaky faucet. That's his craft. Mine included emotional control and manipulation. I remember one day on the *Star Trek* set when a group of actors were listening to a story being told by one of the group. There was a funny ending and everyone laughed. I didn't.

An actress in the group said, "Leonard is in his Spock bag."

I was, deeply into it and that was sometimes a problem. I was like a pressure cooker. Plenty of emotional input, and little or no release. I was so thoroughly immersed in the character that my weekends were a gradual trip back to emotional normalcy. Or as close as I could get to it. By Sunday afternoon I would become aware of a lessening of the Spock presence. I would begin to relax into a somewhat more responsive state.

Sunday night would usually be spent studying lines for
Monday's work. This in itself was the beginning of the return
to character. My wife, Sandi, was very careful never to accept
invitations on a night before work. I need eight hours of sleep.
We socialized on Fridays and Saturdays only. Every other
night, almost without exception, I was asleep by 9:30 P.M. I
usually got home from work between 7 and 7:30 P.M. Often
there were business calls to be made. Then there was little
time left for the family, dinner and study before the 9:30
deadline. I had a phone put in my car so that I could make
some of my calls while driving home.

The morning routine was up at 5:30 A.M., out the door at
6:15, and into the make-up chair at 6:30, breakfast during rest
breaks in the make-up department, and watch that Vulcan
take over my personality in the mirror. The work schedule
was intense. My typical work day was 6:30 A.M. to 6:30 P.M.
Each episode was shot in six working days.

There is a terrible, prevalent misconception that *Star Trek*
was cancelled because it was too costly to produce. This is not
the case. The show was run on a very average budget.
Mission: Impossible which was shooting next door on the
Paramount lot was costing approximately 25 percent more
than *Star Trek*.

The pressure of our schedule and the demands of the work
created interesting side effects. Some were funny, some were
not. I remember sitting in Gene Roddenberry's office one
particular day. I had a brief break and had walked over from
the set. We sat discussing some minor grievance over a script
problem, or whatever. As I spoke to him, I felt the emotions
welling up. My voice began to break, I burst into tears, and
had to leave the room. He must have thought I was crazy.

I had a few other similar incidents. When I could feel it
coming on, I'd get myself to a private place as quickly as
possible, and work it out. It was simply the overflowing of the
pent-up emotions which were not being allowed their natural
outlet in their proper time and place. It was very much like
the scene in "Naked Time" where Spock finds the emotional

outburst happening to him and slips into a private room on the ship to try to rebuild his defenses.

A combination of summer heat and long working hours can create a condition of fatigue on a television production set. "TGIF" or "Thank God It's Friday" is a common expression on the last shooting day of the week. Variations on that include: "It's only two days to Friday," or "Only three days to Friday" or on Monday, "It's only five days to Friday."

In the summer of 1967 on a hot August afternoon, Bill Shatner and I were involved in shooting a scene which included a fight with three or four "heavies" to be followed by some dialogue between Bill and myself before the scene was ended. The fight was, as usual, carefully staged and rehearsed and we were ready with the dialogue so it was time to shoot. We rolled the cameras and proceeded to play the scene and Bill and I managed successfully to do away with the "bad guys" and then proceeded to play our dialogue. As the dialogue proceeded I became aware of a strange rumbling sound. I couldn't tell exactly what it was or where it was coming from and something about the look in Bill's eye told me that he heard it too.

We continued with the dialogue and the intermittent rumbling persisted. Just before the end of the scene I suddenly became aware of what had happened. We managed to complete the scene successfully and my suspicion was verified. One of the stuntmen with whom we had conducted the fight had dropped to the floor "unconscious" when he was supposed to have and then had proceeded to fall asleep. The intermittent rumbling we heard during the course of the dialogue was his snoring.

The *Star Trek* "family" of characters, although set in the 22nd century, is a very easily recognizable group of people when related to other successful TV shows of the past. The most obvious parallels can be drawn with the characters in the *Gunsmoke* cast. For Captain Kirk read Matt Dillon. For Mr. Spock read Chester, the deputy with the bad leg, played by Dennis Weaver, or Festus, played by Ken Curtis. And for Dr.

McCoy, read Doc, played by Milburn Stone. Of course, the style of play and interaction differs because of the nature of the setting and the actor's postures, but the similarities are fairly obvious. In the Chester character, there are obvious physical characteristics, the bad leg which sets him apart as does Spock's pointed ears. In the case of the two doctors, they are almost interchangeable. Both crusty humanists, thinly disguising their devotion to their buddies with a veneer of irascibility.

For Spock, Dr. McCoy, played so successfully by DeForrest Kelley, was the perfect foil. In *Gunsmoke* the humor in the relationship between the doctor and Chester, or later, Festus, was somewhat reversed.

In dealing with Spock, McCoy ventured into areas where others feared to tread. Almost masochistically, he would insult Spock's anatomy, philosophy, or anything else that popped into his brain. Usually, Spock was able to rise to the occasion with a well-placed barb, leaving the doctor fuming. This friendly combat took some time to develop. There was no indication of its possibilities in either of the two pilot films, as I recall, but once established, its value was obvious.

In the first several episodes, the character of Yeoman Rand, played by Grace Lee Whitney, was the direct counterpart to Amanda Blake's "Kitty," the silent, secret love of the leading man. This proved to be clumsy on *Star Trek*. It limited Captain Kirk's potential relationships with other ladies since he would have seemed unfaithful to Miss Rand. She was eliminated to give the amorous Captain more *lebensraum*.

Ironically, the opposite pattern developed in the case of Spock. Although he was theoretically incapable of loving, the female audience notified us very quickly that he was very much loved. This led to the introduction of the "Nurse Chapel" character, played by Majel Barrett.

It was through her character that the female audience could express itself. It was she who worried about Mr. Spock and cooked soup for him. It was she who cared about and quietly loved the Vulcan who couldn't respond.

For the sake of those readers who are interested in astrology, let me report this fact. William Shatner, Captain Kirk on *Star Trek*, is exactly four days older than me. We are both Aries. He was born March 22, 1931 and I on the 26th. We are as unalike as salt and pepper, but on *Star Trek*, I felt we complemented each other in the same way. Most of the time, I could stand the personality of my character next to that of his, and know that the chemistry was right. His romantic, dashing, flamboyant Errol Flynn approach was perfectly suited to my contained, thoughtful Spock. Yes, there were times when I felt that his character was drifting perilously into my territory and mine into his. Each of us, I think, could recognize the value of the areas we vacated and relinquished to the other. But the chemistry was at its best when we functioned in an interlaced pattern each as part of a whole. Frankly, I always felt that the relationship between myself and Jeffrey Hunter, who was originally cast as the Starship Captain, would not have been nearly as successful. Hunter was more reticent and less dramatic in his acting choices, leaving Spock's maneuvering space less clearly defined.

Working from the base of a very comfortable characterization, I had very good instinctive ideas about what was right for Mr. Spock at a given moment. The Spock neck pinch and the Vulcan hand salute were small examples. Shatner had an excellent grasp for the flow of the overall story in a given episode. Where he could more readily find the strengths and weaknesses in the story, act by act, I could best relate to the drama or lack of it in a specific moment.

There were many times, I'm sure, when Gene Roddenberry and our other producers and directors wished we would both simply act. But I believe we helped bring a lot of texture to the shows through these specific personal efforts.

I find it very difficult to play a scene believably unless I believe the scene I'm asked to play. I was never able to lie to a girl in order to achieve a desired goal or effect. I try to keep the same faith with an audience.

When an actor is out of touch with the truth in performance, either because his material has led him astray or he isn't identifying with it, an audience may not know *what* is wrong, but they know that *something* is wrong.

When the truth is being told by the actor and his material, the emotional impact on the audience is complete, and they respond with a resounding "Yes!"

Impact: The Public and The Press

Playing Mr. Spock, standing in his shoes, seeing things from his point of view, living his lifestyle, thinking in his terms, put me into an altered state of consciousness. This condition gave me fresh and exciting insights about myself and the people around me. Many people found this very exciting while some found it threatening. There is a great deal of paranoia in my business. Those people who feel that they must be on the defensive and protect themselves at all times, particularly those with whom I would be working or with whom I had business relationships, projected into Mr. Spock's silence and stoicism a threat to themselves. They felt that I must have been passing judgment on them or scheming against them and was hiding the truth from them in order to disarm them and make them more vulnerable. This often brought about hostile attitudes on their part.

The exact opposite reaction was true in most cases. There is a far-reaching, almost mystical relationship on a nonverbal level between myself, the Spock character and millions of people who relate in a way that is difficult to describe in the language available to us. How else can I explain the fact that on my arrival in Pennsylvania for a college appearance, I stepped into the car which was to take me to the campus and found sitting on the dashboard a beautiful oak leaf with autumn color? I reached out to pick it up and was told by the driver that it had been sent as a greeting by a group of students who were awaiting me at the college, and who thought that I might enjoy having it to experience during the ride. This gentle generous gesture is an example of only one of the endless variety of responses to *Star Trek*, Mr. Spock, and me.

Shortly after the show went on the air, a network of underground communication quickly developed—fan to fan, club to club—which carried current, often up-to-the-minute information about the show and the actors involved. Often their information about our activities has been sophisticated enough to make the CIA look like amateurs.

On my personal appearance trips out of Los Angeles, the details and paperwork are kept to the barest bare minimums. My secretary will hand me my plane ticket with a brief note about the event I'm going to. In most cases I am at the mercy of the individual who will meet me at the other end of the flight. I usually do not know where I will stay or appear except in special situations or cities in which I have requested my favorite hotel.

On one trip to Salt Lake City, I was met at the airport and driven to a local motel. I had been preregistered and was taken directly to my room. As I turned the key in the door, the phone in the room was ringing. I walked in and answered. A young female voice said, "Is this Mr. Nimoy?" I said, "Yes, it is." "Mr. Nimoy, I'm one of your biggest fans. I live in Denver and I just wanted to say hello and tell you how much I enjoy you on *Star Trek*." I was startled, and I asked, "How did you find me?" She said, "I heard you were going to be in Salt Lake City, and I called all the hotels and motels until I got the right one."

I thanked her for calling, and explained that I had to get off the phone since I was due to make an appearance in a few minutes. I hung up, changed clothes quickly, and within five minutes was headed for the door. The phone rang again. I went back, picked it up, and heard: "Mr. Nimoy, my name is Patricia. I'm in Chicago, and I just wanted to say hello." I asked: "How did you find me?" The answer was very simple, "Mary in Denver called me. . . ."

During a break at a personal appearance in New York I was introduced to a young man about 13 or 14 years old. He asked me for an autograph which I gave him. Then he said, "Could I ask you a question?" "Sure. . . ." "How did you beam up into the ship?" I explained briefly that this was an optical effect done through a film dissolve. "Can you really knock somebody out by pinching their neck?" "Only on *Star Trek*," I answered. "What were your ears made of?" "Foam rubber tips stuck on top of my ears with glue." "Did they hurt?" "Sometimes." He scuffled for a moment, then he said, "I don't want to be a hog, but could I have another autograph for my friend?" "Sure," I said, and signed it for him. Then he asked, "Do you have any children?" I answered, "Yes, I have two. They're both older than you. They're in college." He was silent for a moment and then, "I sure wish I had a father like you."

The great range of reaction to the Spock character extends from the oversimplified: "Spock? He's the one with no feelings," to this from a sociology major: ". . . as I see it now, the analysis of Spock will be the central theme of my thesis . . . I find Spock the amalgam of incredible traits. He is an especially contemporary figure as he represents the classic alienated person. Alienation is something we all experience today."

In making the show, the question was: How much depth

can we develop in the stories and the characters, and how consistent can we be?

I've heard that when Picasso was asked to explain the meaning of one of his paintings, he recited the alphabet.

Art, if it is successful, needs no explanation. *Star Trek* and Spock, if they are works of art, can be discussed. But finally the response comes in individual terms. Each viewer sees what is there for him, depending on his frame of reference.

In television, for the sake of mass public penetration, there is a tendency to reduce ideas to their lowest common denominator. A catch phrase or a pithy sentence ". . . a deputy DA has second thoughts about his key witness to a murder." Or ". . . a comedy-drama involving a pregnant student and a physician accused of malpractice."

I was present when a writer presented an idea for a TV show to a major studio executive. The writer was eloquent and enthusiastic. He told his story in rich language, filled with historical and social references. The executive's response was, "That sounds great. But give it to me in a line that I can use in the *TV Guide*."

"Sure I know who Spock is. He's the one with the pointed ears."

Shortly before the debut in September, 1966, I sat with a group of TV editors from various major cities. The meeting took place in Los Angeles, where the press had gathered to meet the stars of new series. They were given complete press kits, and would eventually write in their local papers to inform viewers about the shows and personalities in the new TV season.

I tried hard, very hard, to impress on them the fact that we were doing a very meaningful series. That Spock represented something special. That we were not doing "Lost in Space."

"Tell us about your character." "Well, he comes from a planet called Vulcan. His father is a Vulcan native. His mother was an Earth woman. He's a scientist, extremely logical. Vulcans have learned to control their emotions."

"What does he do?"

"He's the Science Officer on the ship."

"You say he comes from another planet?"

"Yes, Vulcan."

"Is there anything special about him?"

"Well, I already mentioned. . . ."

"No, I mean, does he look like us?"

"Well, . . . ah . . ." The trap was set, and I was about to step into it. I might have made it a lot easier on myself if I had simply jumped in ears first. But somehow I felt that would cheapen the character and the show. How could I bear to reduce my character to a "bottom line" definition?

Ironically, I probably would have gotten more press exposure by simply saying, "I play a man with pointed ears." My fear was that they would never have heard the rest of my story. Now, it was inevitable. They had to know, and I told them.

I took great pains to de-emphasize the physical characteristics. I assured them that this was no cheap gimmick. That our stories would deal with science-fiction concepts at the highest level. I was almost pleading, "Please, don't dismiss us as a far-out fantasy with weird looking creatures." I thought I had made some points.

But the next day, as part of their research, the press group was ushered onto the *Star Trek* stage at Paramount to watch us shoot a scene.

The scene took place in the ship's sick bay. I was lying on an examination table, flat on my back with green blood oozing from my forehead. Dr. McCoy stood anxiously over me trying to recall his training in Vulcan anatomy. The door flew open and in rushed Captain Kirk.

"Spock! What happened?!"

Hoping to be inaudible to the visiting press, I answered, "the creature attacked me, Captain."

On a Sunday afternoon in Toledo, Ohio, I had just finished a personal appearance and was being escorted to my car. There were several fans following with the usual requests for

autographs and one last picture with an instamatic which
might or might not work. Finally the group was satisfied
and we moved on, but I was aware that I was followed by
one particular girl. I turned and said hello and with difficulty she said that she had a couple of questions to ask.
I brought her up alongside of me and told her that I had
to keep moving because I had to get to the airport but
that I would be happy to listen to what she had to say.

She mentioned the fact that she had seen me in the film of
Deathwatch, which was unusual. I asked her where, and she
told me that it had been screened at her drama class in
college. This was a pleasant enough exchange, especially since
after so much work went into the picture, so few people got to
see it. There was obviously more on her mind and the story
came out bit by bit as we walked. She told me that she had a
friend who was a college professor, he had a disease that
affected his vision in one eye. The sight in the eye was almost
gone. Now the doctors told him that there seemed to be a
sympathetic effect taking place in the other eye and that he
would probably lose his vision entirely. She asked me if I had
ever considered the possibility of extending my energies for
medical purposes through physical contact. I said I hadn't and
that I had no idea what she was talking about.

She explained that it might be possible for me to place a
hand on the second eye and arrest the progress of the disease.
She asked me if I would be willing to try it. I was quite
shocked and stopped dead in my tracks. I said, "Dear lady,
what I do is no more than a fiction. I am an actor and only an
actor. I work in a dramatic show playing a character who
seems to have some sort of magical powers. Please understand
this is only a fiction. If there was some way that I could help
your friend, please believe me, I would. But I tell you finally
and flatly I cannot help him in any way." She asked, "Are you
sure?" I answered, "Yes, I am absolutely certain that what I
have just told you are the facts." She said, "Have you ever
tried?" I said, "No, I haven't and I am quite convinced that
there would be no point." At that juncture I think she realized

that I had said my final word. There was a momentary pause and she came back with, "Please think about it."

This kind of encounter saddens me, but it does give me a very powerful and deep insight into the depth of impact of drama of the *Star Trek* kind and characters like Mr. Spock. In cases where a great emotional need develops there is often great desire to find a magical solution. Characters like Spock lend themselves to this fantasy.

I am sure that actors who have played characters like Superman and Batman have also been contacted by people in emotional extremes, or who felt that the actors could be of help through their superhuman abilities to ward off evil and counter hostile forces.

In the Spring of 1967, Isaac Asimov, one of the great science fiction writers of our time, wrote an article for the *TV Guide* about Mr. Spock. The title was "It's Sexy to Be Smart." The article was a very funny, clever piece which suggested that Mr. Spock's attraction to the ladies was due to his superior intelligence. I sent him a note which started a pleasant correspondence.

May 2, 1967

Dear Mr. Asimov:

I am not sure, perhaps times have changed. When I first came to California to start a film career, the current rage was Marlon Brando who had just won the hearts of the American females by playing a stupid, insensitive boor—perhaps you're right, I certainly hope so.

At any rate, the Article was marvelous, and I would expect the response would be excellent.

Many thanks,
Sincerely,

Leonard Nimoy

17 May 1967

Dear Mr. Nimoy,

Thank you for the unexpected pleasure of your letter of the 8th.

Actually, I don't *really* think being unusually intelligent gets more than a small percentage of the ladies, say a few thousand all told. But then, what normal man needs more than a few thousand—especially if all are going to tell.

My fan mail makes it quite clear that what *really* gets the girls is your (or, rather, Mr. Spock's) imperviousness to feminine charm. There is the fascination of trying to break you down that appeals to the hunter instinct in every one of the dear things.

This is the worst news possible for me, for although I am perhaps in the top percentile as far as intelligence is concerned, I am the most pervious man (with respect to feminine charm) that any woman has ever met. I am so laughably simple a conquest that few bother. They just laugh.

Yours,

Isaac Asimov

18 May 1967

Dear Mr. Nimoy,

Sorry to bother you again so quickly, but this will only take a moment. I showed your letter to my young daughter (the one who thought you were dreamy as described in my TV GUIDE article.) I was instantly assaulted.

It seems that in answering I had neglected to ask for a signed photograph of yourself as Mr. Spock. Please forgive my asking but could you have your office send me out a photograph of Mr. Spock, signed, of course, and with "To Robyn" also included.

And one last thing—seriously. See if you can use your influence to keep the *Star Trek* people from *over*emphasizing your imperturbability with respect to women. There should be an occasional hint of hidden fire. Women must be made to feel that their secret fantasy-campaigns to break you down *might* succeed. The absolute certainty of failure would dishearten them.

And I hope the writers and yourself continue to portray Mr. Spock as possessing a clear, dry and underplayed sense of humor. That is *extremely* effective.

(Lest you wonder how I can possibly know how women react to you, I can only explain that my article has drawn fan-mail—and from women, without a single exception.)

Yours,

Isaac Asimov

In 1968, believing we should be out of Viet Nam, I started becoming active in political campaigning.

Leonard Nimoy was an attractive addition at political social action gatherings because of the Spock image. Spock was a character whose time had come. He represented a practical, reasoning voice in a period of dissension and chaos. I spoke at gatherings for Eugene McCarthy, who was the leader of the "dove movement." Aside from McCarthy and other political candidates, I also worked for such organizations as Cesar Chavez's United Farm Workers, Martin Luther King's Southern Christian Leadership Conference and the American Civil Liberties Union. At a meeting of the latter, I first met Dr. Benjamin Spock. I have often been mistakenly referred to as "Dr. Spock," probably because of the fame of the well-known pediatrician. He had been at the forefront in the peace struggle and had been arrested and was awaiting trial for interfering with draft board activities. I introduced myself with, "How do you do. My name is Leonard Nimoy and I play a character called Mr. Spock on the TV series *Star Trek*." He said, "I know. Have you been indicted yet?"

By now the legend of the cancellation of *Star Trek* after two seasons, and it's reinstatement on NBC's schedule for a third year, is widespread. After announcing the cancellation, NBC reported receiving 114,000 pieces of protest mail. Many of those pieces of mail were petitions with hundreds of signatures.

UNPRECEDENTED VIEWER REACTION IN
SUPPORT OF 'STAR TREK' LEADS TO
ON-AIR ANNOUNCEMENT OF SERIES'
SCHEDULING FOR 1968-69

In response to unprecedented viewer reaction in support of the continuation of the NBC Television Network's "Star Trek" series, plans for continuing the series in the fall were announced on NBC-TV immediately following last Friday night's (March 1) episode of the space adventure series. The announcement will be repeated following next Friday's (March 8) program.

From early December to date, NBC has received 114,667 pieces of mail in support of "Star Trek," and 52,151 in the month of February alone.

Immediately after last Friday night's program, the following announcement was made:

"And now an announcement of interest to all viewers of 'Star Trek.' We are pleased to tell you that 'Star Trek' will continue to be seen on NBC Television. We know you will be looking forward to seeing the weekly adventure in space on 'Star Trek.'"

Earlier last week (Feb. 27), in announcing the NBC Television Network's 1968-69 nighttime schedule, Don Durgin, President, NBC-TV, stated that "Star Trek" would be colorcast on a different day and in a new time period—Mondays, 7:30-8:30 p.m. PST; 6:30-7:30 p.m. CST—in the fall. This season the series is being presented Fridays, 8:30-9:30 p.m. PST; 7:30-8:30 p.m. CST.

March 4, 1968

It is interesting to note that NBC reported that *Star Trek* would be scheduled on Mondays, 7:30-8:30 P.M. PST and

6:30–7:30 P.M. CST, in the fall of 1968. Had the network followed through with their intentions, it is very possible that *Star Trek* would still be running as a weekly series today. Instead, the network succumbed to scheduling pressures from other shows and decided to schedule *Star Trek* on Friday night at 10:00 P.M. which signaled the beginning of the end of the series.

In my travels, I constantly meet people who proudly report they sent a letter or signed a petition urging continuation of the show. The feeling is "We fought City Hall and we won." I've never discussed the scheduling or eventual cancellation of the show with any of the network officials. However, Sid Sheinberg, who was in charge of TV production at Universal when I was under contract there in 1972 said, "*Star Trek* followers are fanatic. They'll kill for the show, but there aren't enough of them to make it worthwhile keeping the show on the air."

I must assume that this thinking exists at the network level as well. This, in spite of the fact that the show has been amazingly successful in the syndication market. (Individual stations showing reruns.) Station managers tell me they beat all competition even with the sixth, seventh, eighth reruns of the series. There is a popular notion that actors are paid residuals each time a show is rerun. This is only partly true. We are paid for the first six runs or five reruns. After that, there is no further payment. In the case of *Star Trek*, those residuals ran out a long time ago.

Every once in a while a male member of a lecture audience will raise a hand, and with a gleam in his eye ask me to "tell about the ladies on *Star Trek*." There is no doubt about the fact that we had an extraordinarily lovely and talented array of actresses over the course of the series. Recently a more specific question on the subject has been coming from females.

Question: "In view of the recent women's liberation movement, looking back on *Star Trek*, what is your feeling about the women and the roles which they were given to play?"

Answer: "Looking back on it now, I would have to say that the attitude towards the women in the series was definitely chauvinistic. I can recall only two incidents in which women were actually shown functioning in command roles. One of those was a female captain of a Romulan vessel. It was a direct one-to-one confrontation between her and Mr. Spock. Although Mr. Spock eventually won the day for the *Enterprise,* I believe the female character was handled with dignity and taste. On the other hand, we played an episode in which a female took over the physical body of Captain Kirk in a sort of war between the sexes. In this case the female was finally proven to be inadequate for the command function because of the fact that she was a woman. That particular episode was one writer's personal statement about the comparative capabilities between males and females."

In general, the nature of the clothing and the attitude of the males towards the females in the show would definitely have to be described as sex-object oriented. All I can say is, in spite of the fact that the show was created, produced, and directed by people of enormous sensitivity and vision about the future, the policy makers were almost exclusively men and contemporary men at that.

Science fiction literature for some time has been richly laced with very lush fantasies about women of the future. In the case of *Star Trek* I would have to say that the writers and producers own fantasies were in evidence in the handling of female roles.

I hope this hasn't been too great a source of distress for female viewers of the show. In all fairness I should comment on the fact that my own mail and many of the stories about Mr. Spock that have appeared in various "fan-zines" indicate that a great number of female *Star Trek* viewers have their own fantasies about Mr. Spock as a sex object. The major theme here seems to be that Mr. Spock for some reason, either chemical, medical, physical or whatever, is caught in a situation where his defenses drop and he finds himself in a very amorous mood with a very lovely lady.

The cover of one of these "fan-zines" in particular shows a very well done drawing of Mr. Spock stripped to the waist, his lower portion covered for the most part with a draped toga exposing one bare leg, his hands manacled and a belt from the manacles chaining him to a post. The title boldly reads "Spock Enslaved!" The obvious suggestion is that Spock in this case is a love slave, much in the same way that women have been used for years in erotic or semi-erotic literature. I suppose in this case, turn about is fair play.

At an appearance at Bowling Green University in Ohio, a young lady rose to say, "I'm going to do something for your ego. Are you aware that you are the source of erotic dream material for thousands and thousands of ladies around the world?" I lifted the glass of water that was sitting on the speaker's rostrum and toasted her with, "May all your dreams come true."

The sexual morality of our society tells a story which goes something like this: "Most men would like to make love to most women, most of the time." The one thing that prevents all of this indiscriminate coupling from taking place is the female power to resist. Women are therefore more discriminating, more self-controlled and in general the keepers of the keys to the sexual experience. If it is such a bother to be so attractive to men, I don't quite understand the need for all the dieting, the make-up, the various sprays, the perfumes, the clothing, etc. The name of the game seems to be, "He shall want me, but he shall not have me." If he doesn't want, perhaps a different hair-do, a new dress, a more exotic perfume will do the trick. This can be a very demanding, tiring, expensive and frustrating process. I'm sure it is degrading. Particularly when the female in her moment of triumph is supposed to deliver that final lock-out line which reads, "What kind of girl do you think I am?" or variations thereof.

Down the road comes a stranger. Tall, dark, thoughtful, alien and exotic. Somewhat devilish in appearance. A brilliant mind, the wisdom of a patriarch and oh, so cool. With a raised eyebrow he suggests that he is above game playing and role playing . . . which are hangovers from earth's Victorian age. That he understands and knows about the deepest needs and longings of the earth female. There is no point in trying to dissemble. Spock will not be fooled. Trying to tease, tempt, flirt or be coy would seem inappropriate and ridiculous in the presence of this perception.

SHE: Mr. Spock, may I offer you something to drink? Scotch, bourbon, brandy, a martini?

SPOCK: Madam, my mind is in precisely the condition it should be. I see no reason to alter that condition with stimulants or depressants.

SHE: Would you excuse me, while I slip into something more comfortable?

SPOCK: Since the costume you are now wearing is certainly not functional, and you inform me that it is not comfortable, I fail to comprehend the reason for buying or wearing it.

It just won't work. All the training, all the experience, the preparation and the expense are for naught.

And yet something, somehow must touch this slumbering sexuality. And what if one is successful? The fantasies are endless. There must be stored away here a boundless energy. Pure animal with a brilliant intelligence. Perhaps a touch of childlike naivete kept fresh through rare usage. This could be the journey through the fabled spaces of unknown love and ecstasy. The moments of joy, and torment punctuated with cries of wonder and childlike laughter. Into the abyss of total commitment, relaxation and sheer exhaustion, physical and emotional. Facade after facade of social defense being stripped away until the deepest most secret recesses of the mind have been revealed. And the relief, blessed relief, at being able to drop the burdens of performance and simply exist, free . . . and spent.

It might happen. And this creature might make it happen. He might know that inside me there is a full and rich soul, waiting and hoping. Stored away under layers of idle conversation and empty posturing. A soul locked in the dark for fear of exposure to ridicule. Like a fragile flower encased in steel to be protected against the onslaught of cocktail party thrusts and jabs, clumsy hands and one-track minds.

"Mr. Spock, I offer you the key to my being. If you should care to use it, perhaps you may find there something of value. Something, I hope, special and unique. I will trust your judgment and your capacity for being gentle and kind."

Spock and Me:
The Divided Self

NIMOY: Spock, . . . how does it feel to be popular?

SPOCK: I do not have feelings.

NIMOY: I'm sorry. I didn't mean to offend you.

SPOCK: I am not offended. I understand your tendency to judge me by your human standards. It would however, facilitate matters if you would refrain from doing so.

NIMOY: I'll try . . . Are you aware that you are popular?

SPOCK: I am aware of a certain public interest which exists.

NIMOY: People like you. Do you care about that?

SPOCK: Should I?

NIMOY: Well, I realize that it's not something you would pursue, but being liked is a nice thing.

SPOCK: Popularity can be a corrupting influence. Many of

your political leaders have achieved much popularity and left behind much destruction.

NIMOY: Then, would you rather not be popular?

SPOCK: To be concerned one way or the other is a waste of energy. And popularity does put one in strange company.

NIMOY: How do you mean?

SPOCK: In your culture, popularity may be achieved by bizarre beings and in strange ways. One can achieve popularity by appearing nude in your magazines. Certain animals, dogs, mammals, etc., have become popular through weekly exposure in your television dramas. Would it not be better to honor real achievement?

NIMOY: Can't popularity and achievement go together?

SPOCK: Victor Hugo said, "Popularity? Why it is the very crumbs of greatness."

NIMOY: That sounds pompous.

SPOCK: Possible, but after all, Mr. Hugo was only human.

NIMOY: To be more accurate, Spock, Hugo was only *a* human.

SPOCK: True.

NIMOY: And though there might be some validity to his statement, there are many humans who have expressed many diverse ideas on this and other subjects.

SPOCK: True.

NIMOY: Would you be satisfied if I, as a human, took any random comment from the Vulcan literature as representative of all Vulcan thought on the subject?

SPOCK: To do so would be to deny the usefulness of. . . .

NIMOY: And if you are popular among humans, doesn't that say something positive about the human ability to value a culture and a lifestyle alien to its own?

SPOCK: That does seem logical.

NIMOY: Mr. Spock, coming from you I consider that a great

compliment. From the bottom of my emotional heart
. . . I thank you!

What follows is an excerpt from a speech I delivered to the
Star Trek Convention, New York City, February, 1973:
". . . I have heard from various quarters that Leonard Nimoy
wanted to disassociate himself from *Star Trek,* that Leonard
Nimoy hated *Star Trek,* that Leonard Nimoy didn't want to
have *Star Trek* mentioned around him or ever hear another
joke about pointed ears again. And I will say this, that when
an actor such as myself sets out to play a role as unique and as
special as Spock was, the challenge to us is to try to make
people believe that you are that character. That's what I
consider good acting. And if I have been successful in that,
then I can't complain about that because all of my training as
an actor is related to that end . . . to get an audience to
believe that I am that character. I'm not interested in an
audience watching my performance and seeing the separation
between me and the character. I think we all (the *Star Trek*
cast) feel the same way.

"The whole concept was to create a believable environment in spite of some of the pretty fantastic things that were
going to take place on the show. Therefore, I can not, never
have, and never will complain about identification with the
character. To begin with, because I feel that if that identification has taken place I believe I've done my job as an actor, and
second, because the character is perhaps the most dignified,
most intelligent, most meaningful and most challenging
character that I will ever get to play in my life and I'm very
proud of it!"

That was the truth, but it wasn't really that simple. At the
end of the shooting on the third season I felt finished with *Star
Trek* and Mr. Spock. I thought, "I've had enough of pointed
ears to last me a lifetime." I was very anxious to get away from
the character and the show and move on to other things.
During the next two or three years I began to become more
and more sanguine about my relationship with the character
because *Star Trek* seemed to be fading away and other types

of roles and opportunities were being offered to me.

Then, gradually, during 1971 and 1972 I became aware that *Star Trek* and Mr. Spock were again growing in popularity and were having some negative impact on my opportunities in films and television. Theatre critics who came to see my performances seemed compelled to make some reference to the series and/or the character.

In December of 1971, I went to San Diego, California, to appear at the Old Globe Theatre in a production of *The Man in the Glass Booth*. The theatre had been kind enough to hire Ben Shaktman who had directed me in a production of *Fiddler on the Roof*. The Globe Theatre production department couldn't have been more creative and helpful.

Craig Noel and Adrienne Butler gave us whatever we felt we needed to do a first-rate production. Peggy Kellner, the scenic designer, had done a beautiful job of developing a lovely set and Ben had worked very closely with her to create a multimedia show using rear-screen projection slides.

For me this was a particularly special event. I had always admired the work done at the Globe Theatre and had always wanted to work there as an actor. I also felt that it was close enough to Los Angeles that I was almost working in the theatre at home. The pay was a very small fraction of my normal salary. The size of the theatre and the scale of ticket prices simply does not allow for "star salaries." I was working for three hundred dollars a week and was spending more than that in transportation to and from Los Angeles and maintaining an apartment in San Diego. What made it all worthwhile was that this was a case of knowing what I was doing and why I was doing it.

Glass Booth became a major theatrical and community event in San Diego. Robert Shaw, the author, put together a gut-wrenching piece of material dealing with guilt and vengeance centered on the Second World War and the extermination of Jews in Nazi concentration camps. Being Jewish, I felt very strongly about some of the statements that were being made. There was a small but very vocal group of people in the San Diego Jewish community who felt that the play was anti-Semitic. We were playing to packed houses and standing ovations every night, but I did feel distressed by the negative reaction of this handful of people.

On the other hand I felt that this could be the best kind of community catharsis using theatre as a focal point for an exchange of ideas. Having been contacted by the local Rabbi, we agreed to hold an open seminar session at his Temple to discuss the content and the question of anti-Semitism in the material. Craig Noel, Ben Shaktman and myself appeared at the Temple on a Sunday morning and found approximately 150 people waiting for us. Most of them had seen the play and the reception was very warm and encouraging.

The exchange of ideas was very lively and it became fairly obvious that the overwhelming majority of the people present were Jewish and did not consider the play anti-Semitic. Those few who did were concerned about the showing of the central character as being a Jew who had achieved power through real estate and financial manipulation.

Having very recently played *Fiddler on the Roof*, I had drawn some interesting parallels. I felt that those people, those same people, could identify easily with Tevye in *Fiddler on the Roof* because he represented the image of the poor Jew who didn't make waves and quietly went his way doing what the people in power felt he should do and not arousing any hostility or antagonism. It was interesting to me that in his major character song, "If I Were A Rich Man" he describes all of the fantastic ostentatious things he would do with money if he had it. "I'd build a big tall house with rooms by the dozen right in the middle of the town." "I'd fill my yard with chicks and turkeys and geese, squawking just as noisily as they can, as if to say 'Here lives a wealthy man.' " But Tevye is safe for these particular people because it is assumed that he will never have that money and never will reach that stage of ostentatiousness.

I couldn't help but wonder what might happen if Tevye had arrived in the United States and become as successful as

Robert Shaw's character of Goldman in *The Man in the Glass Booth*. It seems that those same people who had loved him as a poor man would then turn on him with demands that he hide his wealth and function quietly on the lower rungs of society so as not to arouse the hostility of the community towards the rest of the Jews who live there.

The influence of *Star Trek* and Mr. Spock was still very apparent, particularly in the press. Sometimes it would take the form of a passing comment in the body of the piece such as, "Leonard Nimoy, Mr. Spock of the *Star Trek* series, played such and such a role." In other cases the connection was more immediate and direct. One of the San Diego newspapers' critics started his *Glass Booth* review with a banner headline which read, "Nimoy Great Sans Ears."

There were a lot of emotional crosscurrents operating for me at this time. Obviously, the work being offered was coming as a direct result of my impact as Mr. Spock. On the other hand, I was involved in something of a crusade to develop a reputation as an actor with some range.

At this point I went through a definite identity crisis. The question was whether to embrace Mr. Spock or to fight the onslaught of public interest. I realize now that I really had no choice in the matter. Spock and *Star Trek* were very much alive and there wasn't anything that I could do to change that.

I soon found out that the renewed popularity and interest were bringing me more and more offers which, although related to *Star Trek* and Spock, were proving to be very challenging. That being the case, I found that I could simply relax, do the work and go along for the ride.

On February 27, 1975, some seven years after the cancellation of the show, I was asked to appear during *Star Trek* Week at Bowling Green State University, Bowling Green, Ohio. During the course of my stay there, I had some exchanges with some students in a popular culture class:

QUES.: Why do you keep your image of Spock alive? Do you like the character that well?

NIMOY: I don't keep the image of Spock alive. I have had nothing to do with that.

QUES.: I mean, you're coming to Bowling Green as part of the *Star Trek* Week.

NIMOY: Not because I'm keeping the image of Spock alive. You see, the point is, it's happening the other way around. I am invited here because the Spock image is alive, and for me to refuse to come here would not affect, in any way, the life of Mr. Spock. That's the strange thing about it, and that's one of the things that I'm very curious about, and it's interesting that you put the question that way. Because I have done nothing at all to further the life of Mr. Spock. My concern is Leonard Nimoy. Spock is doing great and that's the way it is. That's really the way it is. Now for the first couple of years that they had *Star Trek* conventions cropping up, I didn't go to them. I was really into other things. I was doing *Mission:Impossible* and I was in Europe for almost the entire year in 1972, travelling all over the place, doing all kinds of other things unrelated to Mr. Spock. And then suddenly I said . . . "Look what's happened. Look at that Spock character." I mean it's really nothing that I've had anything to do with. I'm just along for the ride on this trip, and I say I'm here because you, or somebody here has said, "Hey, *Star Trek* and Mr. Spock are popular . . . Let's ask him if he'll come!" So I came.

QUES.: I was just wondering if you feel that it might be financially advantageous to keep the Spock image, whether you are keeping it alive or not, but that it is alive, is good for you?

NIMOY: Let's put it this way. The Spock character is very popular today. Okay. It is creating work for me. Certain kinds of work, certain kinds of appearances, theatrical offers and so forth. So, I'm making money. I'm making a good living, and I have challenging work, and as I say, I really don't believe there's anything I can do, one way or the other, to affect the future of Mr. Spock. That phenomenon has really taken on its own life. If the Spock character were not doing as well, if *Star Trek* had not caught on, I might not be as busy or involved doing this kind of thing, but there's also the possibility that I might be getting some of the offers to do some of those other parts that I'm not getting because of my Spock identity. You see, that's the way the pendulum has swung, and I've nothing to do with it.

QUES.: You're now stereotyped with an image like Spock. I can see where you'd have a problem in trying to get different acting jobs, overcoming that image with a producer or a director. But with yourself, do you have any problem in other jobs, overcoming that image?

NIMOY: With myself . . . ?

QUES.: In your own mind.

NIMOY: No, well . . . in a limited sense, I do. There are times when I start to play another role, a role other than Spock, and discover that perhaps I'm relying, without even being conscious of it, too much on the elements in Spock that were successful and trying to introduce them into the new character. One does tend to want to try to repeat one's success and that is a danger. Once in awhile for the sake of my own exercise I will choose a role that is so totally in opposition to the Spock character that there's no room for that, so that I know that my range is still there, but generally speaking, many of the roles that I'm offered do have Spock-like elements and that's why they're offered to me. Those are dangerous because that's simply a continuation or trying to lift success out of one area and sticking it in another, and it's not really creative, in the true sense. Now for example, I chose to do a play called: *One Flew Over the Cuckoo's Nest*—to play McMurphy, because if there's anybody that's different from Spock, it's McMurphy. Because he's a totally instinctual, gut-level, reactive anti-intellectual character, as opposed to Spock, who is a thinker. That was a very exciting and very gratifying thing for me to do because I really didn't know how successful I would be. I'd catch myself thinking as McMurphy, and I'd say to myself, "Stop thinking," McMurphy doesn't think things out, he feels them out, you see?

For a long time I have been aware that many people would rather meet and talk to Mr. Spock than to Leonard Nimoy. For example at college lecture appearances students who come to hear and see Leonard Nimoy arrive with mixed hopes and expectations. There is curiosity about Nimoy. What does he look like in the flesh? To what extent is he like Spock? In appearance, in manner and in thought. Will they be able to experience the Spock presence, or is this to be a human-to-human contact? They will accept Nimoy respectfully and attentively. They are curious to hear what he has to say about himself, his thoughts and interests, etc. There is probably an ongoing comparison between Nimoy and Spock. A search for those human elements which Nimoy must have replaced with Vulcan characteristics.

Occasionally, Nimoy steps momentarily into the Spock character by choice or accident. The response is a wave of joyous recognition. It is as if Nimoy had stripped away the human facade and given the audience a glimpse of the real person, the Vulcan in the flesh disguised as a human.

Followers of the *Star Trek* show are so attuned to the character traits of Spock that they respond even to the most subtle hints that they are in the presence of the character.

Following the welcoming applause, Nimoy can open a lecture with a simple icebreaker: "You obviously watch a lot of TV," is a rather neutral position establishing a common meeting ground. On the other hand a flat delivery of a Spock line like, "You're a very emotional group of humans," immediately establishes the presence of the extraterrestial and gets a very strong, positive response. They seem to be saying, "Talk Spock."

During a question-and-answer period, the audience delights in seeing or hearing the typical Vulcan response to some of the questions:

QUES. (female): How old are you?

ANSWER (very straight-faced): What did you have in mind? (laughter) The question obviously reflects your need to judge the possible relationship between myself and other beings, possibly even yourself. This represents an illogical human compulsion on your part, based on certain insecurities and a fascination with linear time. It would be better if you humans could rid yourselves of this fixation.

The audience response would seem to suggest a delight in seeing the questioner or even the human race "put down." Particularly where the audience recognizes the question as being childish or fan-like in nature. The position seems to be "Spock should not descend to the level of the questioner. He is not so foolish as to give serious answers on silly or unimportant subjects. In fact, he elevates our thinking by pointing out the foolishness which is inherent in the question."

Among the individuals in the audience there is also a feeling of relief. "I thought that was a silly question and I'm glad Spock agrees with me."

This conversation took place between myself and a young lady who was working on a set of a TV production in which I was involved some years after the making of *Star Trek:*

SHE: In the transactional (TA) sense Spock is pure adult.

NIMOY: The question is why would the adult character of Spock or the pure adult be attractive to people, how would they find it interesting?

SHE: It's very strange . . . it's because underneath I always feel that I detect a deep caring, almost protective.

NIMOY: You mean he protects himself?

SHE: No. He protects the people he is with, particularly humans. That implies caring and loving. That is emotional and not totally adult. His actions seem to feel adult

because he is always rational. He knows what is appropriate here and there . . . he always does the appropriate
thing. But underneath it, I sense that he has. . . .

NIMOY: That he has compassion?

SHE: Yes, there seems to be a caring force which enables him
to be this way.

NIMOY: Of course, he did have an earth-mother, a side which
he has repressed.

SHE: Yes, and perhaps that is the motivating force that comes
out that one feels. That's why I like Spock. Because of
what is hidden . . . What you suspect, what you feel is
there . . . Do you like him?

NIMOY: He's my best friend. He's the only one who understands me.

SHE: (Lots of laughter)

In the early 1960s, I became aware of a very successful
organization known as Synanon, formed in Southern California. This was a self-help group for drug addicts which was
accomplishing more in the cure of drug addiction than could
be boasted by the more widely recognized institutions or the
medical profession. I was teaching acting classes at that time
and was curious about the "Synanon games." This was a group
therapy type of situation. The major difference between it and
other therapy groups being that there was no authority figure.
All the people involved in the group were on the same peer
level and the feeling was that there was no adult or authority
figure to play to.

I became very impressed with the organization and volunteered to conduct some free acting classes at the center.
Synanon has always been very dependent on contributions
from individuals and small groups. No funds were forthcoming from city, state or federal governments. I taught acting
classes weekly for about a year and then remained in close
contact with the organization and some individuals who became close friends.

During the second year of *Star Trek*, my family and I wanted to take a vacation at the beach and we were scouting for an apartment. I mentioned this to one of my friends at Synanon and he suggested that we simply move into the Synanon House for the week. They had taken over a large complex in Santa Monica formerly known as the Del Mar Club. We moved in and spent a very pleasant week in a very unique and exciting environment.

During our stay I was invited to sit in on my first "Synanon game." During the course of the game one of the participants, a black lady who had developed marvelous verbal skills, posed a question to me about my appearance. As a matter of fact I think I should more accurately describe it as an attack. She asked me if I was on some kind of a "freak identity kick." She accused me of appearing like, or trying to appear like, "that Mr. Spock on television." It was my haircut which particularly attracted her attention and she suspected that I was trying to pass myself off as, or look like, Mr. Spock.

It was quite a shock to me. Of course there was nothing I could do about the fact that I looked like Mr. Spock. On that level the whole thing was rather funny. Other participants in the game tried to convince her that I actually was Mr. Spock but she wouldn't hear of it. "Why would Mr. Spock be sitting in on a Synanon game with a bunch of dope fiends?"

More important than the joke involved was the interesting question that it raised. She had accused me of "trying to pass myself off as Mr. Spock." Did that mean that I would rather be Mr. Spock than Leonard Nimoy?

Around Thanksgiving time each year the Hollywood Chamber of Commerce sponsors a "Santa Claus Lane Parade" down Hollywood Boulevard to open the Christmas season. These parades will usually feature many stars of motion pictures and television. The parade route is not very long, I would say approximately a mile or two, but tremendous numbers of people turn out and the sidewalks are quite jammed with parents and youngsters. In the fall of 1966, when *Star Trek* went on the air, Bill Shatner and I received invitations to ride in the parade. We both accepted and arrived at the gathering site and were put into an open convertible.

We moved out onto the street and were immediately welcomed with lots of cheers and enthusiastic shouting. Much of what I heard was, "Hi, Spock" or "What happened to your ears?" which was to become a perennial favorite. Stationed along the route were announcers on public address systems to tell the crowd who to watch for in the upcoming vehicles. After we travelled three or four blocks I heard the voice of one of the announcers booming out over the street. "And here they come now, the stars of *Star Trek*, William Shatner and Leonard Nimsy!" Bill turned to me and said, "You'll probably remember that as long as you live, and maybe you should."

Five years later, I was appearing at the Coconut Grove Playhouse in Miami, Florida. I was descending in the hotel elevator one day and stepped out into the lobby when a very enthusiastic gentleman grabbed me by the arm. "Hey," he said, "look who's here. I know you, I watch you on television all the time. I've got to have your autograph!" As we fished for pen and paper he spotted a friend of his walking through the lobby. "Charlie," he yelled, "come here quick . . . look who's here." Charlie approached just as I was about to sign my name to the piece of paper the gentleman had come up with. "Charlie," said my new acquaintance, "Do you know who this is? You see him all the time on television. Charlie, this here is Kreskin." I signed *Kreskin* to the piece of paper, shook hands with the two gentlemen and left.

Three years after that incident, I was doing some shopping in a market in Hickory, North Carolina. The lady who was waiting on me had recognized me when I came in and was extremely charming. As we did our business she insisted on introducing me individually to all the help in the store. Usually, these introductions are done in a testing process: "John, do you recognize this man?" or, "Mary, do you watch television?" The embarrassed individual is then forced to stare at me as an object of curiosity wondering who this person might be. Sometimes the recognition is immediate. On the other hand sometimes people are shocked to find "Mr. Spock" standing in their little market in Hickory, North Carolina. In this particular case, the response from one of the ladies was, "Why, of course I recognize him . . . my son watches him all the time." She reached out to shake my hand and said, "You're Leonard Spock!"

A Family Affair

From 1950, when I did my first film job, to 1966, when we started shooting *Star Trek*, I felt like a professional orphan. The studios represented homes, and those actors who worked there under contract were part of the immediate "family." Those of us who "jobbed in" for a few days work, were at best, distant cousins or merely temporary guests who were allowed to visit but didn't actually belong.

In sixteen years I never had a studio job that lasted longer than two weeks. My dressing rooms and parking places, if I got one at all, had temporary name cards, easily removed the day the job was over. I never realized how deeply I needed to be accepted into one of those "families."

When it finally happened, when *Star Trek* went into production and I was asked to come to stay, I was in for quite a surprise. In many ways the acceptance was everything I expected. I cheerily waved to the guard at the front gate every day and got a very warm welcome in response. Drivers ahead or behind me had to stop, state their business and hope that the gate would swing open for them.

My name plate was secured to the dressing room door with reassuring screws and my name was painted on my parking space!

My fellow artists were all my brothers and sisters and I had several parent figures: directors, producers and studio heads.

But there are tensions and misunderstandings in the closest families. When I had need of goods and services which I felt were necessary to do my job properly I naively assumed that the parents to whom I submitted my requests would see the need and react appropriately!

Not so. Fathers very often reject a son's request as being "not necessary," "too expensive," "if I do it for you, I have to do it for all the others," etc., etc.

There is a little item which establishes the boundaries of the relationship between a studio and its actors. It's known as a contract. Before it is signed, everything is negotiable. Salary, billing, dressing room, expense money, phones, parking spots . . . everything! After it is signed, goodwill takes over.

When the Spock character became as successful as it did, I felt I was a son who was doing his share to carry the family load. The studio legal department saw me as a menace. "He's getting popular and he's going to want more than he contracted for. That's trouble."

Much later I was to learn to anticipate all my reasonable needs and have them built into the contracts to avoid misunderstandings. But in the meantime we played some interesting games.

Ten days after the show went on the air I was handed my first batch of fan mail. It consisted of about eight or ten letters which pleased me greatly. Over the years I had received an occasional fan letter, and at one time had inquiries from

people who wanted to start a fan club. However, it was
obvious during those times that there was never enough
excitement about any particular job or group of jobs I had
done to warrant that kind of fan activity. I was very unprepared for the onslaught that was about to take place.

I sat down during a lunch hour that day and personally
responded to each of the letters and personally signed each of
the photographs with a handwritten note.

Several days later another batch of mail was brought—this
time it consisted of about forty or fifty letters. These I did
during breaks in shooting and during a couple of lunch hours.
About a week later three or four hundred letters arrived. The
personal touch was now out of the question.

Within a couple of months my mail was being delivered in
sacks and it tallied up to approximately ten thousand pieces of
mail per month. Fan clubs were springing up like weeds all
over the country. This presented a new series of problems
since there were expenses involved in handling all these
matters.

The following is a series of memos resulting from the cost
of handling fan mail and fan club communications:

Desilu Productions Inc.
Inter-Department Communication

TO: LEONARD NIMOY   DATE: JUNE 12, 1967
FROM: ED PERLSTEIN   SUBJECT: FAN MAIL

Dear Leonard:

For the past several weeks I have been consulted with
respect to the operation in regard to your personally
handling your fan mail and have iterated myself many
times with regard to the agreement that I made with
respect to our obligations to you in this connection. For
purposes of clarification to you and the others receiving
copies of this memo, I would like to iterate the agreement that was made.

1. Desilu, in addition to your compensation, agrees to
pay you $100 towards your secretary and equipment

needs for your personally handling the fan mail.

2. All equipment is to be furnished by you other than that specifically enumerated herein below. We agree to furnish you the following:

a. The photographs of you that we select.

b. All postage with respect to fan mail which the studio would normally cover under its existing fan mail facilities.

c. Stationery designated by Desilu for fan mail and not your own personal unapproved stationery. Envelopes will be furnished by Desilu.

It is not intended nor was it specifically agreed that we would furnish you with *pencils, pens,* etc. which we assumed you would furnish yourself as we also contemplated that you would furnish your own typewriter and other equipment.

From the requests that you have made and which I have rejected and which we will charge you for items such as staplers, staples, pens, pencils, pencil sharpener, memo pads, special stationery, applications for membership in Leonard Nimoy Fan Club and any expense in connection with fan clubs is something that we are not responsible for as this goes beyond the STAR TREK series and which I personally consider a personal item of expense.

This is not a witch-hunt but rather a business letter asserting rights on behalf of profit participants, including the network, the producer of the show, Desilu Studios and other profit participants. None of the profit participants or interested members have raised nor are aware of your requests nor have they raised any specific beef concerning your requests and concerning the charges. As I said, there have been many inquiries regarding proper classification and charges and it has come to the point where in my opinion this memo is necessary.

If you have any questions concerning this memo, pro or con, then I would welcome your reply and for this purpose I invite you to use, free of charge, an inter-office memo.

I urge you once again to consider this memo in the vein it was intended for clarification of those charges which are properly to be absorbed by Desilu and that which is to be considered personal and your personal items of expense.

cc: Herb Solow
    Gene Roddenberry
    Gene Coon
    Bob Justman
    Leo Pepin
    Bill Eatherly
    Shirley Stahnke
    Bob Winslow
    Dick Sternberg

TO: ED PERLSTEIN   DATE: June 13, 1967
FROM: LEONARD NIMOY   RE: FAN MAIL

Dear Ed:

I want to thank you very much for taking the time to send me your memo clarifying—or attempting to clarify our agreement as regards to: fan mail, supplies, etc. My impression is that there are two (2) primary issues raised in your memo, and I should like to deal with them forthwith so that we may arrive at a satisfactory understanding.

The first issue seems to be that which has to do with the provision of pens, pencils, etc. I hasten to assure you that my secretary and I have managed to steal enough pens and pencils from various offices around the studio, so we will no longer need to make requests in this area for some time.

The second area deals with those expenses and I quote from your memo: ". . . in connection with fan clubs . . . that we are not responsible for, as this goes beyond the Star Trek Series and which I personally consider a personal item of expense." In this area we may have to create a sub-division, since not all of the 160 fan clubs could, in all fairness, be considered completely personal. I list herewith a few examples of some of the clubs which might fall out of the "personal" category:

"Crew of the Enterprise"—Mobile, Alabama
"Star Trek Association"—Los Angeles, Calif.
"Spock"—Los Angeles, Calif.

"The Enterprise II"—Oceanside, Calif.
"The Star Trek Club"—Jackson Heights, New York
"Enterprise, Inc."—Great Neck, New York
"Star Trek"—Elmira, N.Y.
"Vulcanian Enterprises"—Brooklyn, N.Y.
"Star Trekkers"—Brooklyn, N.Y.

Those are some examples of the clubs which I feel fall most predominantly in the Star Trek area, and can not in all fairness be considered "personal" clubs.

Then there are those which I feel we should split. For example:

"Nimoy Enterprise"—San Jose, Calif.
"Leonard 'Spock' Nimoy Fans, Inc."—B.C. Canada
"Yomin Enterprises"—Pontiac, Michigan
(The name of the ship in this case being spelled forward and my name being spelled backward—perhaps, we ought to go for a 75% vs. 25% split of the expense.)

In fairness to all parties involved may I suggest that we arrange for a periodic audit of the fan club files in order to determine where the expenses should rightfully fall. Perhaps, Price-Waterhouse would be available for such an audit, and we could arrange for a dramatic presentation of the findings in a sealed envelope.

Yours for fair and equitable allocation of expenses,
LEONARD NIMOY

At this point, Bob Justman, our production manager and eventual co-producer got into the act. Bob has a brilliant imagination and a lovely sense of humor, but let him speak for himself:

TO: ED PERLSTEIN   DATE: June 14, 1967
FROM: BOB JUSTMAN   SUBJECT: FAN MAIL

Dear Ed:

I have received copies of correspondence between Leonard Nimoy and yourself recently. With respect to Mr. Nimoy's memo of June 13th, I should like to report to you that I have noticed that pens and pencils have been disappearing from my office at a phenomenal rate. I don't have proof, so I don't think that I can logically accuse anyone of these thefts. However, I staked out my office the other night in an attempt to identify the guilty party.

Unhappily, some unknown assailant sneaked up behind me and clamped a fiercely vise-like grip upon me somewhere between my neck and shoulder. I lost consciousness within a split second and did not awaken until several minutes later. To my dismay, I noted that there were more supplies missing from my office.

Whoever attacked me and stole my supplies must have been endowed with a quite superior sense of hearing, as I am certain that I made no noise and, in fact, was quite careful to breathe as lightly as possible.

There is one very strange fact which has emerged from this incident. I had rather cleverly concealed a naked razor blade within my pencil box, so that whoever would be stealing my pencils would have an opportunity to slice open his or her finger. Upon investigating my now empty pencil box, I discovered a slight amount of the oddest green liquid present on the razor blade and around the bottom of the pencil box. I can't imagine what it can be. It certainly isn't blood, as we all know that human blood is red.

Incidentally, getting back to fan mail. This past season I have received three fan letters. I answered them post-haste. Please send me fifteen cents to cover postage.

Sincerely,

BOB JUSTMAN

cc: Leonard Nimoy
    Herb Solow
    Gene Roddenberry
    Gene Coon

TO: ED PERLSTEIN   DATE: JUNE 15, 1967
FROM: SPOCK   RE: FIRST AID

Dear Mr. Perlstein:

I should like to file a complaint about the first aid facilities here at the studio.

It seems that late one night last week, while doing some very important work in my office I had a minor accident and cut a finger. I went to the first aid office only to discover that they are closed after shooting hours. I think it highly illogical to assume that accidents only take place during shooting hours.

What can be done?

SPOCK

CC: Herb Solow
Gene Roddenberry
Gene Coon
Bob Justman

Within a month after the show went on the air I had telephone problems. There was one phone on the sound stage and between cast and crew there were about 50 people receiving and making calls. I was getting calls for press interviews and personal appearances from all over the country. It wasn't always possible for me to come to the phone because most of the time we were rehearsing and shooting. The message slips would pile up and when I got a break I would go to the phone and try to return some of the calls only to find people waiting in line. The next closest phone was a pay booth on the studio street outside the sound stage. This meant precious minutes wasted going to and from the pay phone and very often it too was occupied with people talking.

I spoke to the production manager about my problem and requested that the studio put in a telephone into my trailer dressing room which was on the sound stage. He told me that he would pass on my request and I heard nothing about it for the next week. I raised the question again and was told that Herb Solow, head of TV production for the studio, was aware of my request and wanted to discuss it with me.

I assumed that this meant there was a financial question involved. There was no telephone deal in my contract. Therefore, I would be required to pay for it myself. I decided not to bother Solow. He was a very busy man and this was a minor matter. I told the production manager that involving Solow would be unnecessary, I would pay for the phone myself.

Another week went by and I heard nothing. The situation was getting critical. Much of my phone business was to eastern cities. By the time I got finished with the day's shooting it was far too late to get in touch with the people on the East Coast.

I raised the subject again, and once more was told that I would have to discuss it with Solow. He finally came to my dressing room to state his position. There were several actors on the lot who wanted phones. I could not be allowed to have one since it would set a precedent. Other actors would want to follow suit. "Herb," I said, "there seems to be a breakdown in communications. I have already agreed to pay for the phone myself." "I know that," he answered, "but I can't let you have the phone." I asked him to explain. He said, "If the other actors find out you have it, they'll want one. I'll tell them you're paying for it, but they won't believe me. There'll be a lot of hard feelings."

Eventually I was able to persuade Herb that the studio was losing money if I had to go to the pay phone while the company waited for me. I got the phone. And I paid for it myself.

In the spring of 1967 we started production on the second season of *Star Trek* shows. I hired Teresa Victor to take care of my fan mail on a full-time basis. It soon became obvious that it was physically impossible for her to take care of my mail and handle other office responsibilities as well. We turned the fan mail over to a service which specializes in that work. During the hiatus between the first and second seasons we had renegotiated my contract with the studio. The new terms included a raise in salary, and the studio was to provide me with a permanent dressing room furnished as an office. During the first season I had only the portable trailer on the sound stage. Teresa moved into the office and assumed her duties. All calls were put through to her and she coordinated my activities. Travel plans, requests for personal appearances, photo sessions and interviews with the press, etc.

The office consisted of two small rooms each approximately twelve feet square with a small bathroom in between.

There was a window in each room, but no cross ventilation. As summer came on and the temperature rose, the room became unbearably hot. We needed an air conditioner.

I approached Morris Chapnick who was an assistant and troubleshooter for Herb Solow, the studio head. Morris promised "to check into it." Several days went by. "Morris, what about my air conditioner?"

"I checked the contract," he said, "and it doesn't call for anything except office furnishings." "Morris," I said, "that's true, there's nothing in the contract about an air conditioner, but the office is practically useless without it." He said, "I'll see what I can do." A few days later some workmen arrived and installed a small exhaust fan in the top of one window. It was completely ineffective.

A couple days later the heat was intense. I told Teresa to lay down on the floor and play unconscious. Then I called the studio nurse. When she arrived I told her I'd found Teresa on the floor, obviously passed out from the heat. The nurse applied some cold compresses and Teresa "revived." Then I called Chapnick and told him of the incident. He checked with the studio nurse. In two days we had an air conditioner.

All of the foregoing could easily come under the heading of "Fun and Games." There was a lot of intense emotion connected with it at the time, but in retrospect it all seems rather silly. Much more important was the ongoing effort to successfully exchange ideas within the family with regard to the nature and quality of the scripts and, of course in my case, with particular emphasis on the Spock character.

The following are samples of memos I sent to various producers during the production years. They deal with some specific script problems, and more important, my constant and increasing concern with the preservation of the best and the most important elements of Spock.

The response to these memos, if indeed any was forthcoming, was usually in the form of conversation or a specific script change. There were many more discussions on character and script than these few memos would indicate. Particularly during the first two years there were constant discussions with

Gene Roddenberry and eventually, Gene Coon. Most of
these were fruitful. During the third season, when Roddenberry and Coon had departed the series, the communication
between me and the story editor and producer was not nearly
as successful. It finally reached the point where communication between them and me came to a total standstill. The final
memo in this chapter clearly indicates the depth of my
frustration.

TO: GENE RODDENBERRY   DATE: MAY 18, 1967
CC: Gene Coon
FROM: LEONARD NIMOY   RE: "Amok Time"

Dear Gene:

Have just finished reading the yellow cover version of
"Amok Time" and am very, very happy with it. I think
that the story very successfully involves all of our central
characters in strong and meaningful relationships.
There's a strong line of suspense and emotional contact
throughout the script.

Whatever criticisms I do have relate primarily to the
latter part of the script. On Page 51, Kirk says to McCoy,
"You said, this fight might save his life." I don't feel that
this idea is completely clear. That is, in what way can
Kirk save the life of Spock by fighting him? From Scene
#87 into Scene #105, we lose touch with Spock and
therefore do not have any indication of what his attitude
is about the fight; or more specifically about the fact that
he is to fight Kirk since Kirk has been chosen as the
challenger. We have had interplay between Kirk and
McCoy showing their feelings about Kirk having to fight
Spock but no reference to Spock's attitude or his point of
view. I feel this needs to be developed so that we can get
some insight as to what Spock's condition is. Is he so far
out of it that he doesn't even know who he's fighting? Or,
does he feel torn by the idea of having to fight Kirk?

Beginning on Page 64, approaching the tag of the show, I
feel that we may be cheating ourselves of a more powerful payoff to what has been essentially a very strong
script. A suggestion would be that because of the nature
of Spock's emotional experience with Kirk in the sick
bay, that perhaps the two of them be in there alone. I

The first film role as "Chief Kojouski" in *Queen for a Day*.   Robert
Stillman Productions, 1950.

The title role as the young fighter in *Kid Monk Baroni*.
Realart, 1952.

Leonard Nimoy as "Jules le Franc"; Paul Mazursky as "Maurice" (foreground); Michael Forest as "Greeneyes" (far corner); Robert Ellenstein as "The Guard"; in Jean Genet's *Deathwatch*. The Deathwatch Co., 1966.

The first role as an "alien," *Visit to a Small Planet.* Pheasant Run Playhouse, Chicago, Illinois, 1968.

Leonard Nimoy as
"Zastro the Magician"
in "The Falcon."
Mission: Impossible,
Paramount Studios,
1969.

In the title role of
"The Robot" in
Mission: Impossible,
Paramount Studios,
1969.

In Spain starring with Yul Brynner and Richard Crenna in
Catlow. MGM, 1971.

Leonard Nimoy as "Tevye" in *Fiddler on the Roof*. Touring New York,
Ohio and Massachusetts in 1971.

The Old Globe Theatre production of *The Man in the Glass Booth* with Leonard Nimoy in the title role.

In *Oliver*, Melody Top Theatre Milwaukee, 1972.

As "King Arthur" in *Camelot* for summer theatres in Massachusetts, 1973.

In *The King and I* at Melody Top, Milwaukee, 1974.

Leonard Nimoy as "McMurphy" in
One Flew over the Cuckoo's Nest.
Little Theatre on the Square,
Sullivan, Illinois, 1974.

As the mad emperor in *Caligula.*
St. Edward's University, Austin,
Texas, 1975.

Leonard Nimoy as the Holmes character in *The Interior Motive*.
Kentucky Educational TV, 1975.

feel uneasy about Spock showing that emotion over Kirk's supposed death in the presence of McCoy and Christine. I think that Spock would go off and do that by himself. But, since he believes Kirk to be dead I think we have an opportunity for him to express that emotion in the presence of the supposedly dead Kirk.

The tag of the show too, I believe is cheated by the fact that Spock goes off on a rather lame mission (to get some soup . . . I believe). Couldn't we wrap up more powerfully with a strong three scene between Kirk, Spock and McCoy?

All in all, a very gratifying script to read and am looking forward with great pleasure to shooting it.

Sincerely,

LEONARD NIMOY

TO: GENE RODDENBERRY

DATE: February 21, 1968

FROM: Leonard Nimoy   RE: Mr. Spock/Star Trek

Dear Gene:

It gives me great pleasure to know that it is you sitting behind the Producer's desk talking the stories with the writers for the new season. Deep inside me, I feel that your talent, your taste, and your efforts, will again make "Star Trek" and "Mr. Spock" a fulfilling experience, in spite of the amazingly complex pressures which exist in this project. In short, I do believe that our goals are the same, and I would like to take this opportunity to express a few thoughts pertaining to *Mr. Spock.*

During the first season "Mr. Spock" *was* the First Officer of the Enterprise, intelligent and resourceful in command when the occasion demanded it. He *was* the Science Officer of the Enterprise, using a vast background of knowledge and capable of correlating information in the amazingly logical and computor like way in order to make scientific determinations. He *was*, sometimes right, sometimes wrong, but could definitely be relied upon to have an individual and unique point of view. His loyalty often *was* dramatized by circumstances, rather than simple lip service. His Vulcan soul may someday burn in hell for the things he did and said to support his human friend, but he bit his tongue and did it because that was his duty as he saw it. He sometimes saved a life, or once or twice even the Enterprise, because he as a Vulcan was able to accomplish something which was beyond human action. He *was* precise, very mysterious, physically powerful, and even mystical. I could go on and on, but suffice it to say that in a brief time there were built into this character far more dimensions than one finds in a group of characters put together on television.

Public response indicated that we had done a *groovy* thing.

The Scientists admired his logical precise and scientific mind. The Hippies dug his cool and his mysticism. The kids revelled in his strength and his sharp dry wit, to say nothing of his fascinating ears.

SECOND SEASON

I shall try and be fair. There were some very gratifying moments. But looking back from this vantage point, Spock seems to have added up to:
1) A raised eye-brow
2) "Fascinating" . . . "Logical" . . . "Illogical" . . .
3) The "Spock pinch"
4) "I am sorry Captain, but at the present time, and with the present information, I am unable to give you anything more specific than that" . . .
5) "The planet is Class M, Captain, not unlike your Earth, and capable of supporting human life" . . .
6) Some comedy sketch dialogue between Spock and McCoy, often petty in nature, and usually capped with "Gentlemen, will you please stop the bickering amongst yourselves, I need answers not arguments." (Captain Kirk)

Gene, I can't tell you how many times scenes were introduced with: Kirk and Spock enter, followed by several pages of dialogue during which we cut to Spock for a raised eyebrow, and finally Kirk and Spock leave. There were times when the writer had so completely forgotten that he had introduced Mr. Spock into the scene that he forgot to have Spock make the exit with Kirk, and tag the scene simply with *Kirk leaves.*

It would be as if Shakespeare had written "To be or not
to be . . ." to be played by two characters instead of one.
Often, Bill and I found ourselves equivocating over the
problem of the piece during the second and third acts, in
spite of the fact that we felt the audience must be way
ahead of us, but we couldn't arrive at a solution because
it was too early in the play. For example: Briefing room
scenes seemed to be designed to kill time by explaining
to each other that we did not know what was going on, or
what to do about it.

Captain Kirk: To be . . .
Mr. Spock: . . .or not to be . . .
Dr. McCoy: Yes, that is the question . . .
Captain Kirk: I've made my decision . . .
Dr. McCoy (angrily): Jim, you've endangered thousands
                of lives . . .
Mr. Spock: (His eyebrows slowly rise . . .)

Believe me, I know that piece and harmony are vital in a
series situation, but must it be reduced to this:

Spock enters bridge, approaches Captain's chair . . .

Spock: Captain, I believe I found the . . .
Kirk: The answer, Mr. Spock?
Spock: Yes Captain, I am convinced that the planet is
                . . .
Kirk: Infested, Mr. Spock?
Spock: Yes, Captain, with a rare and unique disease
                which is capable of . . .
Kirk: Making itself invisible to our sensors, Mr. Spock.
Spock: Precisely, Captain . . .
Kirk: Exactly what I had expected, Mr. Spock. . . Good
                work. What are the odds, Mr. Spock?
Spock: I would say, approximately 47.3 to 1, Captain.
Kirk: I'll take that chance . . . Prepare phasers, Mr.
                Sulu.

Please, Gene, let Captain Kirk be a giant among men, let
him be the best damned Captain in the fleet, let him be
the best combat officer in the fleet, let him be the
greatest lover in the fleet, let him be capable of emerg-
ing unscathed from a brawl with five men twice his size,
but above all let him be a LEADER, which to me means
letting your subordinates keep their dignity.

TO: GENE RODDENBERRY
TO: GENE COON
TO: BOB JUSTMAN
TO: JOE PEVNI
FROM: LEONARD NIMOY RE: "DEADLY YEARS"

I would like to refer you to the fact that in the past we have established that Vulcan life span is approximately 3 times that of humans. That being the case Spock being on the high side of 50 (page 23), leaves some question as to whether that age is meaningful, perhaps the best thing to do is to drop the Vulcan age entirely, or be much more specific about it, and actually point up the fact that Spock may be aging to the point of 100 years or more, which would bring him more in line with some of the aging processes that are taking place with the other people.

Act III—Page 40

I believe we're missing a very valuable opportunity in having Captain Stocker interrogate Kirk and the other witnesses at Kirk's hearing. This could in effect be a very powerful or dramatic scene between Kirk and Spock, since it is strongly established that Spock does not want the hearing to take place at all, and we'd have some excellent drama to play, if with that sub-text working, Spock is forced not only to attend, but to actually prosecute.

The marvelous payoff available here is that having successfully prosecuted as he "logically" must, Spock refuses to take command as Stocker suggests. This would very dramatically emphasize Spock's "logical" position in prosecuting and his loyal position in refusing to replace the Captain.

Scene #63

Again, should be a 'Kirk-Spock' scene. In the prosecution we have, in effect, Barney Greenwald prosecuting Captain Queeg as he rightfully must, in spite of the fact that he believes in Queeg and does not want to destroy the man. Now, we have an opportunity to play a marvelously fresh facet of the relationship between Kirk and Spock. Kirk, the aging father figure, who is shocked and hurt by Spock who is kind of a son figure who has turned on his father. In this scene we get a chance to play "Willy Loman" and "Biff," Willy in a paranoid condition (Captain Kirk) taking everything personally. Spock, trying to calm him, and wishing there were some way he could point out to him that there is nothing personal, no personal betrayal involved.

Page 71—Scene 87

Spock and McCoy exit. McCoy to give Spock a shot in sick bay.

Page 72

Kirk turns to Spock and says, "Mr. Spock, take over." Sorry Captain, Spock no here, he gone to sick bay.

TO: FRED FRIEBERGER   DATE: MAY 6, 1968
CC: BOB JUSTMAN
FROM: Leonard Nimoy SUBJECT: "The Last Gunfight"

Dear Fred:

As per our phone conversation, here are whatever ideas I could put together before leaving. Aside from the other problems discussed, I believe that "Spock" should start working on constructing his device (whatever that is going to be), no later than scene #31. Perhaps on Page 18, where "Kirk" says, "I have no intention of letting a bunch of primitives kill my people and myself." At this point, if not earlier, I believe that we must begin to introduce the concept that we are here because of a scientific or telepathic force, and that we must find a scientific or telepathic way in which to combat it. If "Kirk" begins to initiate his relationship activity at this point, "Spock" should begin to initiate his scientific activity.

To me, it makes more sense that "Spock" would be trying to build a communicator, or some kind of electronic signalling device, rather than a phaser. I think that his primary aim should be to get out of here, rather than to win a fight, since we must accept that we can not do that. If we continue to play the idea that we could win this fight then we deny the whole premise which is, that we are the "Clantons" and we will lose in any fight.

Perhaps this idea could be dramatized in "Spock" wanting to use the gunpowder from the bullets in order to build his equipment. The others might be interested in maintaining the use of their weapons, while "Spock" points out the futility of weapons in trying to beat the history involved.

Scene #46: The horse gets through the force field, and "Kirk" is knocked off. I didn't get a response about this on the phone, and I must point out that a force field is something that we have established as simply being an invisible wall. It does not choose between man and beast. I think we take a very dangerous license here in terms of the future, for the sake of what I consider at best, a mediocre joke.

A new thought, if the sets are to be facades, then shouldn't we suspect or even understand that the whole thing is an illusion and, therefore, try earlier on in some way to telepathically or through self-hypnosis or whatever, eliminate the illusion?

Also, how about time? Should we consider it as real in terms of what the clock says, or should we give some thought to that area in terms of possibly even setting the clock back or trying to adjust it in order to change the flow of events?

Question: If the sets are not real, it therefore follows that we know that the whole thing is an illusion, therefore, this is not the real gunfight at the "O.K. Corral," therefore, we do not necessarily have to die in the gunfight. Maybe we have to deal with that, in order to maintain the suspense.

Scene #109: "Kirk" instructs "Spock" to eliminate only the reality of the bullets. It becomes clear that he wants the rest of the stuff preserved, specifically so that we can engage in a brawl with the "Earps." As you get to know me better, you'll find that this thing, this type of thing, irks me very much. I am bored by the fights we get into, and can bear them only if they are thoroughly motivated and integrated into the script. In this case, we might just as well have the "Captain" say, "Just eliminate the bullets, "Spock," because I want to have a big fight here."

Question: If the "Melkotians" are powerful enough to create an environment in which "Spock's" device fails, why do they let us win the fight with the "Earps"?

I am sorry I can't be more helpful. It seems in this case I must choose the role of "The Devil's Advocate"! Wish you the best, and will be in touch when I get back.

Peace!

Leonard Nimoy

TO: Gene Roddenberry, Doug Cramer DATE: October 15, 1968
    Fred Freiberger, John Reynolds
FROM: LEONARD NIMOY

GENTLEMEN:

During the first season of "Star Trek," a character named "Mr. Spock" was established in the series. This character had pointed ears, extremely high intelligence, was capable of brilliant leaps of deductive logic, could contact people's minds, could tick off data about Earth, space, time, etc. as though he had memorized libraries on the subject, was extremely powerful physically, had a great deal of pride, and a few other things, which in general made him a smart ass.

Now we all know that nobody, but *nobody* likes a smart ass, and above all a continuing character in a TV series must not only be liked, but well liked! Therefore, I can well understand the efforts this season to change this character's image, so that he will be more acceptable to the American public.

Now we are embarked on re-doing a show that we did during the first season when it was originally entitled, "Dagger of the Mind," with guest star, James Gregory. A story of a planet which supports a mental institution. The title has been very cleverly disguised, and we are now calling it, "Whom Gods Destroy." Since evidently the show was effective the first time around, we have managed to retain much of the story line for the second shooting.

I note one major difference which is evidently indicative of the drastic change in the "Spock" character. In "Dagger of the Mind," "Spock" picked up some valuable information by mind-melding with a man whose mind was terribly disturbed, and "Spock" was able to gather information from him only through the mind-to-mind contact which Vulcans are capable of. In our current episode, "Spock" is confronted with what would seem to be a rather simplistic situation. He walks into a room, phaser in hand, and is confronted by two "Kirks." One is obviously his real Captain and the other is an imposter. Question: Can Spock handle the situation using his deductive logic, the phaser in his hand, his previous experiences with Kirk, his mind-meld, or any of the other imaginative techniques that a smart ass Vulcan would normally use? The answer is: NO.

Not only is he unable to cleverly, dramatically, and fascinatingly arrive at a solution, he also proves to be a lousy gun hand, since he allows the two men to become embroiled in a brawl while he stands there holding a phaser, not sure whether he should shoot one or both, or maybe just let them fight it out and "hope that the best man wins."

Now I'm given to understand that a fight between the two "Kirks" is absolutely vital to our series. I guess I can understand that from a production point of view. It seems that most series are cutting down, or cutting out violence, and I guess "Star Trek" will corner the market with this kind of sub-rosa activity.

My primary interest in contacting you gentlemen, is my concern over my lack of experience in playing dummies. Perhaps you could arrange to get me educated in this area. Maybe if I watched some "Blondie" episodes and watched "Dagwood" as a role model I could pick up some pointers. Or better still, I could get right to the bottom line by wearing some braids and feathers and learning to grunt, "Ugh, Kimosabee"?

Any suggestions?

Hopefully,

Leonard Nimoy

Why?

Today there are active *Star Trek* fan clubs throughout the world and several *Star Trek* conventions scheduled throughout the United States each year. The interest in the show does not seem to diminish. Why? There is an ancient Chinese curse, exquisite in its irony, which says, "May you live in interesting times."

The *Star Trek* years, during and since the filming of the show, have been years of dramatic ferment, political polarization, sexual revolution, drug abuse and a multitude of other turbulent events. The characters in the *Star Trek* series are a family. Tied to each other through common interests and loyalty. Diverse in their backgrounds, there is a deep mutual respect for each others talents and individuality. In this atmosphere, there is a place for any individual capable of making a contribution of value. People are judged on their merit without regard to origins or personal philosophies. There is a healthy common goal. To explore, to find answers, solutions to troubling problems and to share their solutions with all intelligent life.

There is hope. In the 22nd century, we exist. We have survived the atomic and hydrogen age. We have contacted intelligent life on other planets. We have joined in an inter-galactic federation to work together for the common good. We are useful to ourselves and to others, we respect truth, and recognize that beauty exists in many diverse and interesting forms. We have survived the wasting and near destruction of earth's natural resources. We fight dictatorship and political demagoguery, and we win. It is a good place to be and a good time to be there.

Violence is de-emphasized and certainly not glorified. Life is precious. The prime directive, although we dangerously skirted the edges several times, states that we shall not interfere with the natural development of any society. No doubt there are many young people who would like to exist in that environment and hopefully make a contribution to it.

Recently, I noticed that the city of Detroit had set a record of dubious distinction by going 48 hours without a homicide. Mark Twain's beloved Mississippi River is suspected of being contaminated with cancer-producing water, food prices have skyrocketed, young men murder their entire families for no apparent reason. Victims of terrorist attacks in the Middle East scream for revenge through desecration of the bodies of the attackers. A major military figure raises the spectre of anti-Semitism, sounding very much like the Fascists of the 1930s. In Viet Nam we left our bodies, our blood, and our self-respect. George Orwell's *1984* concepts of "doublethink" and "newspeak" have crept into our society. Public faith in political leaders is shattered. Science finds easier funding for destructive weapons than for cures. Who can care? Who has the stamina and the emotional fortitude to continue to hope that conditions will right themselves? Is it any wonder that millions stay home on Election Day?

I was stopped one day by a lady in a subway station in New York City. She said, "Excuse me, sir, but I have keen powers of observation. Aren't you the man on that series in space?" I agreed that I was. She said, "It's a very fine show, but some of the stories are too fanciful. You should make them more down-home." I guess she avoided "down-to-earth" because it might have come off as a bad pun. But *Star Trek* was down-to-earth. If the problems we dealt with on the show were examined beyond the most superficial glance, they would be discovered to be earth problems. Overpopulation, pollution, racism, destruction of natural resources, blind fear of anything new or foreign, unemployment, drug abuse, the machine and electronic device replacing the worker, etc., etc. If these stories were told in obvious earth terms, that lady could not have withstood the onslaught.

In the face of all this, wouldn't it be wonderful if the U.S.S. *Enterprise* actually existed? If there were another, parallel universe populated by people who have been through all this and could help us get through it? How many other TV series could successfully serve as the basis for a course of study in philosophy or sociology as *Star Trek* has?

At its best, *Star Trek* was *about* something. It carried a thematic thrust missing in most TV shows. Yes, there was adventure, futuristic weapons, romance and other entertaining elements. But most of the shows, and certainly the series, were about *something*, revealing and dealing with the flaws of existence as a means of ennobling life.

Why? Why does a generation raised under the influence of Dr. Spock relate to Mr. Spock? Is Spock embraced and welcomed because mankind is troubled by the march of events? Here is an ET of superior intelligence and abilities. Capable of making difficult decisions free of ego and pressure, and emotional needs. Dealing (supposedly) only with the facts in each case and the logical conclusions. The period in which Spock arrived was one of polarization over major political and social issues. The war in Viet Nam, the drug culture, the black revolution, assassinations, etc. Perhaps Spock represents a wise father figure to whom humans could turn for solutions to thorny problems. In many cases humans are torn between doing the right thing, and doing the expedient thing. "I know what's right, but if I do that, what will my neighbors say, what effect will it have on my family? What will it cost me?" Spock seems fo be free of these tensions. In the Vulcan culture, one simply does what is right.

Perhaps a connection with another fictional character would be useful. Since I played Spock, I have been offered the role of Sherlock Holmes on several occasions. In fact, Gene Roddenberry suggested it as a series idea for me several years ago. I finally did the Holmes character in January of 1975 in a fifteen minute program produced by Kentucky Educational Television to be used in an Earth-Space Science series for junior high school students. The film was produced in Lexington, Kentucky and featured the characters of Sherlock Holmes and Dr. Watson. The idea was very clever. To use the Holmes and Watson characters and their reknowned capabilities as detectives to demonstrate to the students how a scientist uses inductive reasoning in scientific exploration. A globe is delivered to Holmes' apartment and he is challenged to discover the contents and nature of its interior without breaking the surface.

The film was directed by George Rasmussen and the script, written by Richard L. Smith, was a joy to play. As much as any other element involved in the making of the decision to play it was a comparison written by Smith delineating the similarities and differences between Mr. Spock and Sherlock Holmes. This was included with the script which was first sent to me and read as follows:

> Sherlock Holmes is first and last a creature of intellect. Moreover, his interests are narrowly specialized. His nature bears certain similarities to the character of Mr. Spock, but the differences are important.
>
> For example, although both men are intellectual and unemotional, the reasons are different. Spock has subjugated his emotions through iron discipline while, in Holmes' case, they have atrophied through inattention.

> Spock is always phlegmatic, but Holmes is often nervous and agitated. His nerves almost pop out of his skin at times, and we can always read his thoughts in his face. Holmes' temperament is basically artistic, although his intellect is entirely objective and rational. Unlike Spock, Holmes could never be part of a team, especially in a secondary role.
>
> Spock, we sense, is a man of profound conflict and tension, the human side of his nature may have been crushed and imprisoned but we watch him, fascinated, and wait for it to some day break free.
>
> There is no conflict within Sherlock Holmes. The artistic and scientific sides of his nature complement each other. Everything that does not serve his single purpose has been allowed to wither away. In his child-like simplicity, he is like some Nobel Laureate in Physics. Holmes likes and respects Watson, but he recognizes the differences between them. Their relation is that of a man and his dog, one which may have saved his life on occasion.

For me the key connection between Spock and Holmes lies in their ability to solve problems, to cut through rhetoric, lies, deception, and fantasy. TV detectives are very popular. Audiences have faith in them. Jack Webb's Sergeant Joe Friday reduced useless conversation with a withering Spock-like line, "Just give us the facts, Ma'am." Perhaps Spock, with his superhuman intellect, is the greatest detective of them all. Because we know that Spock is part human and we suspect him of being compassionate, possibly even a secret humanist, we feel safe in placing our fate in his hands. Certainly he would never make a decision which, though logical, would be anti-human.

In Albert Camus' dramatized version of the Caligula story, the mad emperor resorts to "logic" as a means of alleviating the economic problems of the state. As the need for money arises, wealthy people are simply executed and their money confiscated.

Logic alone might someday dictate the extermination of millions of innocent people in order to relieve overpopulation, food shortages and other ecological problems. In that case, we would turn to Spock the scientist and hope that he would find brilliant scientific ways to fulfill mankind's needs rather than eliminate portions of mankind.

So this particular ET, or type of ET, is superior in his decision-making abilities and in his scientific knowledge. But we trust that he will apply these superior assets to our benefit. Maybe he'll even answer some important questions for us.

NIMOY: Spock, what is life?

SPOCK: A state of being.

NIMOY: Let me put the question another way: Why is there life?

SPOCK: Yours or mine?

NIMOY: Anyone's.

SPOCK: You've missed my point . . .

NIMOY: Which?

SPOCK: "Yours or mine" . . . I was trying to suggest something.

NIMOY: You've lost me . . .

SPOCK: How can that be? To have lost something is to be unaware of where it is. You are still here.

NIMOY: It's just an expression. I meant I don't understand.

SPOCK: Your question is based on a personal conjecture. "Why is life" suggests that there is a single reason for all of life.

NIMOY: Is that wrong?

SPOCK: Is that necessary?

NIMOY: Many people are troubled by this question. They feel somehow that their lives would be enriched if they knew why they are here.

SPOCK: Are you religious?

NIMOY: I think so.

SPOCK: Then, perhaps you are here because God wants you to be.

NIMOY (stunned): Spock, I'm really surprised to hear you say that. Do you mean it?

SPOCK: Why does that matter? We are investigating possibilities. Does that one appeal to you?

NIMOY: Possibly. At times.

SPOCK: Do you believe in the concept of service to mankind?

NIMOY: I think so.

SPOCK: Then perhaps you are here to be of service.

NIMOY: Suppose neither of those possibilities satisfies a particular individual?

SPOCK: We've only suggested two. Aren't the possibilities endless? And why do you feel responsible for supplying the answer for everyone? Have you chosen that as your reason for existence?

NIMOY: Then each person has to find his own?

SPOCK: "Has to . . ." That would seem to suggest an emotional need, to which I find it difficult to relate.

NIMOY: Are you going to hide behind that mask of logic?

SPOCK: Are you angry with me?

The teenager coping with the fiercely complex problems of adolescence often feels very much alone. His friends or peers are understanding, but they too are faced with the same problems and have no solutions. They can only commiserate. Parents claim to have the answers, but they are short on patience and understanding. Then, too, the child-parent competition makes it difficult for the child to accept the parent's solutions. They seem old-fashioned, or at best, out of touch with contemporary attitudes. Too often, the parent's advice is couched in very emotional terms. Spock easily resolves this dilemma. He has superior insight. He can quickly understand the nature of the problem. He has studied the human race. He is a pure authority on the subject. He has no axe to grind because he is so totally secure. He certainly can not be accused of being old-fashioned. He is future. He can be compassionate in his judgment and dispassionate in his help. To the young female, there is no sexual threat. Spock is asexual. She need not fear that he will take advantage of her. In fact, quite the contrary. He probably becomes an object of sexual fantasy because he is at once safe and challenging. This would be even more true with more experienced females.

I was doing some homework one day. Without being conscious of doing it, I was quietly singing a song by Jacques Brel:

> If we only have love
> We can reach those in pain
> We can heal all our wounds
> We can use our own names.
>
> If we only have love
> We can melt all the guns
> And then give a new world
> To our daughters and sons . . .

I was startled by Spock's voice from behind me. "What is that song?"

NIMOY: Well, it's a poetic idea. It suggests that we could all get along with each other if there is common love.

SPOCK: Do you believe in this concept as a possibility?

NIMOY: I see nothing wrong with believing that mankind could someday find a real brotherhood.

SPOCK: There is no need to be defensive. . . .

NIMOY: Spock, there are some things which we humans care about that may seem strange, even ridiculous to you. What's wrong with a little hopeful poetry?

SPOCK: It is not the poetry I am curious about. I understand it. It scans fairly well, and some of the images are quite lovely. Poetry has an important place in Vulcan literature.

NIMOY: Then what's your point?

SPOCK: The poet suggests that love can stand alone as an emotional entity.

NIMOY: Where does he do that?

SPOCK: "If we only have love, we can melt all the guns."

NIMOY: What he means is that if people love each other, there wouldn't be any more wars.

SPOCK: Illogical.

NIMOY: Why?

SPOCK: War is the result of a breakdown in reason. It is an emotional confrontation. To eliminate war, it would be necessary to eliminate emotion. Love, being an emotion, would thereby be eliminated as well.

NIMOY: Are you saying that we can't have love *and* reason?

SPOCK: Most human literature would suggest that reason disappears in the presence of love.

NIMOY: Under the influence of a drug, you once fell in love.

SPOCK: True . . .

NIMOY: When it was over, I heard you say, "I was happy for the first time in my life . . ."

SPOCK: Your typically human assumption is that I had lived a deprived life, and have now at least had an insight into a blissful state.

NIMOY: Isn't that what you meant?

SPOCK: Not necessarily. My statement can also be interpreted to mean, "I have had an experience peculiar to the human race."

NIMOY: That's not what it sounded like when you said it.

SPOCK: That is a matter for individual interpretation.

NIMOY: Didn't you like the experience?

SPOCK: I can understand that you would *want* me to like it.

NIMOY: Why?

SPOCK: Because you want me to be like you. To value the

things you value and to give support and credence to your life style.

NIMOY (losing patience): Look Spock, all of this is very interesting. But you did say you were happy. By definition that's a pleasant and emotional experience.

SPOCK: I know this is difficult for you. But please try to understand. I said, "I was happy for the first time in my life," in the same sense that a visitor to America might say, "I had a hamburger for the first time in my life." Of course, most Americans would like to hear him add ". . . and I loved it."

NIMOY: Spock, you're impossible.

SPOCK: Are you angry with me?

Spock is a good man to have around. He is brilliant, dignified, loyal and cool. In a crisis where humans stumble, Spock functions with logical efficiency. He is extremely honest and incorruptible. He seems to be compassionate, although he would deny it because that borders on emotionalism.

There is a suspicion that Spock has knowledge which could be very helpful to a troubled humanity. I have been contacted by metaphysical organizations. One group told me that I had been chosen for the Spock role because I was a carrier of ideas, concepts of which I myself might not be aware. That my real function in the series was to prepare mankind for the future and to relieve public tensions about phenomena which were bound to come. This particular group communed in the Nevada desert and had personal and direct contact with extraterrestrials who visited them and took members of the group on short rides on their spacecraft. They could reveal themselves to me, they said, because I would be capable of accepting and understanding. However, they felt the public would be hostile and needed further education through roles like mine.

Spock is a safe and comforting, even desirable resolution of the extraterrestrial question. Many people have gone to great lengths in writing to me about the effect he has had on their lives. They often tell movingly that he demonstrated a dignified way for the individual to function in what, for many, is a hostile society. If there are extraterrestrials and if we are to encounter them or be visited by them, most people would be relieved if they were all like Spock.

Young people are fascinated by the "Spock neck pinch," a grip which applied by a Vulcan to the neck and shoulders renders a human unconscious. Most preteenagers want a demonstration, preferably on a friend. One can't help but wonder what the reaction would be if Spock were one of a group of Vulcans on board the *Enterprise*. The existence of one Vulcan whom we all know, trust and love, is all well and good. But suppose there were several Vulcans bound together in a political action group? "One is O.K., but when his friends and relatives move in . . . there goes the neighborhood."

It is easy to forget that Spock was created by humans. And if he does in fact represent elevated concepts of life, its value and its meaning, then those elevated concepts must be credited to the human race. Personally I find this an enormously exciting challenge—to try to live up to the broader vision and deeper perception that I helped build into this fictional character.

Instant Replays

All *Star Trek* followers have their favorite episodes. In discussing this with people connected with the show I discovered that we of course have our favorites too. The choices are arrived at for personal reasons. In some cases there is an overlap where we all agree that a particular episode or group of episodes stood out as "special." In other cases the favorites have to do with some personal identification with the content or perhaps because that particular episode was especially meaningful in the development of the particular character we played.

At the risk of slighting some very fine writers and directors, and chancing the possibility that I will overlook some titles which are personal favorites of the fans, I'll try here to give a brief summary list of those shows which mean the most to me today.

"This Side of Paradise," written by D. C. Fontana, dealt with the loss of the work ethic on an earth colony. The inhabitants have been infected by a spore which is native to the planet, which has eliminated their motivation for accomplishment. They are happy just to indulge themselves by passing the time in a placid state. Mr. Spock is affected by the spores in quite a different way. He becomes reacquainted with a young lady that he has known for some years and when he is exposed to the spores his conscious defenses are reduced to the point where he becomes aware that he has loved this lady and still does.

With the exception of Captain Kirk, all of the crew members, including Mr. Spock, would be quite ready to abandon their duties on the *Enterprise* and remain in this blissful state on the planet. Of course, the crew must get back to work and again pick up their duties to the space service and to society. In a tender parting scene Mr. Spock's first name was almost revealed. When Leila, the young lady in question, points out to Spock that she doesn't know his first name, Spock responds with, "You couldn't pronounce it."

This is a very special episode for me for obvious reasons and particularly because, where Spock was so totally adult in most of his attitudes and reactions throughout the series, this episode provided a chance to expose the complete child within. We saw him loving, picnicking, romping and literally swinging playfully in the trees. It was a total exposure of the internal Spock that so many people have always suspected was there.

"City on the Edge of Forever" was a beautifully constructed love story for Captain Kirk, written by Harlan Ellison. The female role was played by Joan Collins. The story took place in the earth 1930s during the Depression. On a trip back in time Captain Kirk meets and falls in love with a very lovely social worker. The story is exquisitely constructed in its tragic design in that the Captain and the girl are deeply in love and we discover that the girl is to die in a street accident.

Knowing that she is to die, of course the Captain is
tempted to save her but we realize that if he does this, the
flow of future time will be disrupted. Therefore, the participants in the love story are caught in a classic tragic construction. The story was beautifully written and wonderfully produced and directed. I also happen to believe that it was one of
Bill Shatner's finest performances.

"Amok Time," a lovely, poetic script by Theodore
Sturgeon, was a very special story again for Mr. Spock, in that
it was the first time we visited his home planet of Vulcan. It
was great fun to explore the possibilities of seeing Mr. Spock
in his own culture among his peers. The storyline dealt with
the fact that once every seven years Vulcans come into the
mating season and Spock's time had come. He was on his way
home to fulfill a match which had been made for him as a
youngster. The story was rich in Vulcan ritual and was the first
time the Vulcan hand salute was used. This consisted of
holding the hand up, palm outward, the thumb outstretched
with a separation between the second and third fingers. This
salute was introduced during the moment when Spock first
arrives on the planet and is met by T'Pau, the Vulcan mat-
riarch played by Celia Lovsky. She is carried in on a sedan
chair and verbal greetings are exchanged.

At this point I felt that there was an opportunity to
establish something a little special in the way of a Vulcan
greeting. The greeting that I chose came from my Orthodox
Jewish background. The hand symbol is that used by the
Kohanim, who are the priests of the Hebrews, who bless the
congregation during the High Holiday services. Saying, "May
the Lord turn his countenance unto you and give you peace,
etc." While doing so they extend both hands out toward the
congregation in the configuration that I described.

There are many interpretations of this symbol but the one
which seems most obvious is that the hand, when held in that
shape, forms the shape of the Hebrew letter *Shin*. This is the
first letter in the word *Shadai*, which is the name of the
Almighty. Therefore, the Kohanim are using this symbol of
the Almighty's name in blessing the congregation. This then

became the appropriate exchange when Vulcans were to greet on *Star Trek* in the future. It has also been picked up by thousands of fans and I am greeted with the Vulcan hand salute wherever I travel.

Another landmark episode would have to be "Dagger of the Mind." Not because it was in itself what I would consider a major *Star Trek* episode, but because it was the first time that we introduced a very special talent for Mr. Spock . . . the Vulcan mind-meld. This was a brilliant innovation by Gene Roddenberry. In the episode we were dealing with an emotionally disturbed individual who had some information that we needed. Because of his unstable condition he was unable to give us the information verbally. Rather than have a long, torturous and dull dialogue sequence, Gene conceived the idea that Spock, through a hand contact to the individual's face, would be able to meld his own mind with that of the subject and get past the disturbances which were at the conscious level. In this way he could probe into the subject's mind and read out the necessary information.

It was established that this was a difficult and taxing process for Spock. It was another one of those magic effects which captured the imagination of the audience. Unfortunately, later in the series this particular technique was used in a less dramatic form which made it seem almost like an everyday occurence, thereby somewhat reducing the magic and the tension of the moment. Too often a writer will use a device to get himself out of a difficult plot situation. However, the idea was extremely effective and "Dagger of the Mind" served to introduce it.

Of course, a list of favorites would be incomplete, to say the least, without mention of "The Menagerie." This was again a sample of Gene Roddenberry's working at his best. It was a two-part episode constructed essentially out of material which had been shot as the first pilot for *Star Trek*. The story very simply dealt with Spock hijacking the *Enterprise* in an effort to return his former Captain to Talos IV—Captain Pike was paralyzed as a result of a radiation accident. On Talos IV he will be able to live out a full life in spite of his physical limitations because the Talosians have a highly developed capability for cerebral illusions.

Roddenberry took the original pilot material and reconstructed it with some additional shooting to include the present day crew of the *Enterprise* and created a pair of *Star Trek* episodes which were at least among the best, if not actually the best of the shows, we ever put on the air. I doubt that any other television series or even television special has ever achieved the level of production, texture and ideas that were contained in this pair of shows.

"Devil in the Dark" was an episode written by the late Gene Coon, who functioned as a producer and writer for the series for approximately a year. In this episode some miners have been killed by an unknown attacker while working in the tunnels below the planet surface where they are extracting a valuable mineral. Their fear has escalated to hysteria. Investigation reveals that they have been unwittingly destroying the eggs of a native of the planet, a silicone creature known as a Horta. The creature has been responding in the only way she knows how in an effort to protect her young.

The major thrust of the story was that we fear the unknown and the unexplored in much the same way that people in ancient times felt the earth was flat and were convinced that explorers would fall off the edges if they went too far. The successful relationship eventually established between the Horta and the miners suggests that when both sides come to know each others' needs and each others' intent it is often possible for them to work together harmoniously. In a crucial scene in the plot, Mr. Spock communicates with the Horta creature through the Vulcan mind-meld. Through this procedure Mr. Spock discovers who and what the creature is and the story is brought to a successful resolution. This is probably the only time in my life that I've ever been asked to establish communication with a living rock.

"The Enemy Within," written by Richard Matheson, would be another one of those that must be mentioned here because it was a landmark episode again for Spock. This was the episode in which the Vulcan neck pinch, described in a previous chapter, was first introduced.

These are just a few of the ones which most frequently and most specifically come to mind. Obviously, there are many other shows which were excellent for the series as well as for the Spock character. It goes without saying for example, that "Miri," "The Naked Time," and so many others were really excellent scripts, beautifully executed. All I've tried to do here is outline some of those which are my lasting personal favorites for very subjective reasons.

I was finishing a question and answer session after a lecture one night in Asheville, North Carolina. I said, "One last question," and looked around at the raised hands to make a choice and the audience started chanting, "The little boy, the little boy." There was a small boy standing in the aisle who had had his hand raised for some time and I hadn't called on him. I did, and his question was, "Would you tell me what's really happening when you beam down to the planet and back up on to the ship?" The place burst into applause because evidently the question had been on the minds of the entire audience. Young and old alike had wanted to hear the answer.

The "beaming down" process is the procedure we use to leave the ship and arrive on a planet surface and then to return to the ship. The process was the result of a creative idea growing out of a problem. It was decided during the preproduction stages that it would be too expensive to show the ship landing or taking off from planets. Therefore, the *Enterprise* would never land. Of course, it was necessary to get us on to planet surfaces and back to the ship so the transportation process was created by Gene Roddenberry.

It is a very simple process technically. It can be shot very quickly and is not terribly expensive to execute. Therefore, it was useful for us. But something about it has captured the imagination of audiences. Theoretically we are converting matter, in this case the human body, into energy, transporting that energy elsewhere and reconverting it to matter. In actual fact we're using a very simple process known as a film dissolve. Anybody who watches a motion picture or TV show, will see a film dissolve take place and probably not be conscious of it. It is that moment when a scene comes to an end and gradually fades out while the next scene is at the same time fading in. So, what the audience is seeing is an overlapping of the end of one scene and the beginning of the next. This same process is applied in the "transporter effect." The film is shot of the empty transporter room and then some footage shot with the characters in the transporter room. By overlapping these two pieces of film/footage the effect of appearing and disappearing is created visually with a minimum of cost and time expanded. If the empty room is shown first, then we fade into the scene with the footage with the characters present and get the effect of the actors "appearing." If the footage is used in reverse, that is, the characters in the room, and then the empty room, and gradually dissolve from one to the other the effect of disappearing is created. The same is true on the planet surface. A simple and classic demonstration of the old adage that "necessity is the mother of invention."

There is no doubt in my mind that, with the possible exception of the bridge set, visitors to the *Star Trek* stages were usually surprised and let down by what they saw. A few small sections of corridor, the Captain's quarters, sickbay, transporter room, etc. The quality of the set design by Matt Jeffries, and the photography by Jerry Finnerman and later Al Francis, created a look on the TV screen that led visitors to expect to walk on board a mammoth ship. Their work, together with the talents of the special effects department and the sound effects people, created an amazingly believable environment.

To my knowledge, the sets were dismantled and discarded to make space available for other TV productions.

Mission to *Mission*

The work on *Star Trek* lasted for three seasons: 1966, 1967
and 1968. I felt that the best work had been done during the
first two seasons and that the scripts and production during
the third year did not at all reflect the highest quality of the
show to say the least.

I had very mixed emotions about the possibility of continuing to play Mr. Spock. My feelings were that there would
have to be some very drastic changes in order to bring the
series back up to its original quality.

There were two major problem areas. One was story, the
other was character. In the area of story, I felt that our scripts
had drifted to the point where they no longer represented the
excellent science fiction that we had achieved when we were
at our best. For the most part I felt the stories were excuses to
get us into and out of danger within the given one hour

109

period. When we were really cooking we had dealt with some very exciting and some very profound and even important ideas, relative to the human condition. For the most part, our third year stories were devoid of ideas.

In the area of character, a gradual blurring had taken place. Where there had originally been an opportunity for very distinct characterizations and the character interplay, there was now an erosion which destroyed the clearly defined characters, particularly among the three central figures, Captain Kirk, Mr. Spock and Dr. McCoy. The simple, bottom-line truth was the show was no longer fun to play.

My contract with Paramount required two more years of service. However I felt strongly enough about these problems at that time that I would have resisted coming back to work under the conditions which existed. This would have meant suspension from my contract at Paramount and possibly even an injunction against my working elsewhere in films or television until the matter had been legally settled. None of that was very important to me at the time, nor is it now. If I had simply chosen in my life "to work for a living" I could have found very secure work in other areas much earlier in life. Right or wrong, drama for me is a kind of spiritual crusade. When all the elements are in place and functioning properly I get a sense of well-being which makes me feel that all is right with the world. To watch the gradual erosion of the quality of the *Star Trek* show was just too painful for me to bear, regardless of the cost.

Fortunately, or unfortunately, whichever the case may be, the confrontation with the studio became unnecessary when NBC cancelled the show at the end of the third season. I received the news with very mixed feelings. Of course, it would have been very exciting to go into a fourth season with some fresh ideas and the possibility of recapturing the best of what we had had. On the other hand, since that seemed extremely difficult because of various circumstances, I felt that perhaps it was best that we leave the show behind and move on to other things.

An actor working in a series is equivalent to a cog in the studio machinery. The relationship may be full of extreme emotion ranging from love to hate, but the actor is considered vital to the smooth functioning of the studio's daily activity. A studio is loathe to remove an actor from an ongoing series. There have been rare and special cases where this has been done because the relationship became completely untenable. Much effort will be made to keep the relationship intact, rather than take a chance on the potential negative public effect of removing or replacing a series actor.

When a series is finished the actor is about as necessary to the studio as a third hump on a camel. He is simply taking up space. In early April of 1969 it became obvious that *Star Trek* was not going to be picked up for the following season. I was still occupying office space with my girl Friday, Teresa Victor. I received the inevitable call from Ed Milkis at Paramount who informed that since *Star Trek* would not be continuing they would be needing my space and would like to have some indication of when I could vacate. I told Ed that I had a couple of short trips out of town coming up and that as soon as I came back I would be looking for new quarters. He was very congenial and agreed that if it were a matter of two or three weeks there would be no problem. Within a few days I got another call from Ed. This time the situation was much more urgent.

It seemed a new writer had been hired to work on the *Mission: Impossible* series and would be needing office space immediately. How quickly could I get off the lot? I pointed out to Ed that I hadn't yet had time to decide where I would locate and that if we could stick to our original agreement I could still be out in the appointed period of time. As tactfully as he could, Ed made it obvious that they wanted my space immediately. The next day, in order to facilitate my removal from the lot the transportation department sent over a small van and two workmen. They loaded all of my personal belongings into the van and we precipitiously moved all of my equipment and supplies to Teresa's home where they would be stored until we found a new office space from which to function. It was obvious that I was now a third hump.

Star Trek was finished and I had absolutely no plans for the future. I was very interested in the possibility of broadening my base as an actor by doing a variety of roles which would move me into new areas of exploration and public recognition.

Trouble was brewing in the *Mission: Impossible* company. *Mission* and *Star Trek* were sister shows. They had both been sold by Paramount at exactly the same time and had started on the air side-by-side, and were actually produced on adjoining sound stages during the three years that had just passed. While *Star Trek* had started off with a somewhat respectable rating picture, it had gradually been moved into weaker and weaker time slots until finally in the third season it was put on the air on Friday night at 10:00 P.M. which was the worst of all possible time periods for the show. Our potential mass audience of young people were out doing their weekend things. Wherever possible, people who were dating arranged either to meet early and watch the show together or to meet after the show was over. However, this wasn't enough. Many Friday night activities made it physically impossible for people to be at home when *Star Trek* was on the air.

Mission: Impossible, on the other hand, started out very poorly in the ratings and I would have thought had a very dismal chance of survival. The difference was that someone at CBS had high hopes for the show and had faith in its future. They moved it into better and better time slots until somewhere in the second or third season it began to catch hold and find its audience. Once that happened it was obvious that the show was in for a good long run.

At the end of the third season, Martin Landau and Barbara Bain were involved in some very difficult negotiations with Paramount. Landau had been working on a season-to-season contract, and was free to negotiate for whatever he thought were his best interests for the season to come. By the time it became clear that *Star Trek* was to be cancelled, it was also evident that Landau and his wife, Barbara Bain, were not going to successfully complete their negotiations for a fourth season on *Mission: Impossible*. Having reached an impasse, and having decided to move off in another direction, the studio contacted my agent about the possibility of my moving into the *Mission: Impossible* show.

There were several aspects of the deal which were especially attractive. In the first place it meant that I would be back on the air immediately in the new fall season playing a wide variety of characters as Landau had been doing for the previous three years. This meant that at least for myself I would be able to reexplore and reexamine my range as a character actor. In a sense it was like going back to the beginnings when I found acting to be such a delightful adventure. The opportunity to play all kinds of people had always intrigued me. In addition, there was the fact that *Mission: Impossible* was already a successfully established show. While this removed some of the challenge of being involved in the creation of a new series, there was compensation in the fact that the format of the show was secure and I would be free to work comfortably within that successful format. The offer from Paramount was quite generous in comparison to what I had been earning on the *Star Trek* show. Having worked on adjoining stages for three years I felt quite comfortable with the *Mission* company and looked forward to working with them.

I approached the situation very carefully. There had been many lessons to be learned about working in a series which had been made very clear to me during the making of *Star Trek*. Between my agent and Paramount and myself, we worked out a formula whereby I could "test the waters" so to speak, in the *Mission: Impossible* situation before plunging in. Paramount was to give me a commitment to do eight episodes on *M:I*. The scripts were to be submitted to me for my approval and based on my availability. This is what I would consider an ideal situation for an actor. It simply means that Paramount had to offer me the opportunity to play eight of their scripts at a predetermined and generous price. I, in turn, could do the scripts if I liked them and if they did not conflict with other commitments. On that basis I went to work.

I called Ed Milkis, who had been so helpful in facilitating my movement off the lot after the cancellation of *Star Trek*. Ed was now aware that we had just made a deal for *Mission: Impossible* and immediately sent the truck and two drivers to move me back onto the lot. I laughingly commented to him that we might have saved a couple of moves if they had let me stay on the lot just a bit longer. It was now only about three weeks since they had moved me out. Ed put it very simply, "We didn't love you then, but we love you now."

The first scripts offered were two scripts to be done in a two-parter. While the scripts were not the best I had ever read, they did give me an opportunity to play three or four different characters and to get my feet wet in the immediate challenge of playing various roles, disguises, dialects and so forth. While we were still at work shooting the two-parter, Paramount submitted the next script to me, and it was a beauty. I was to play a character rather loosely based on the character of Che Guevera—the revolutionary leader. The script was well constructed, and the character, being fairly well-developed, was very enticing. I accepted the job and started doing as much research as time would allow in order to get some feeling for an indepth approach to the character. For wardrobe and make-up we gathered photographs of Che and of course, there was the inevitable Cuban cigar. I had a great time with it. During the shooting of the show the footage must have reflected the fun that I was having. At this point Paramount and CBS evidently agreed that they wanted me to make a fuller commitment to the series, and asked me again to sign a long-term contract. We agreed and made a four-year deal.

For the next year and a half I settled into the business of being a man of a thousand faces. It was fun for a while. I was back into researching the characters, studying dialects, experimenting with make-ups and so forth. In some cases we were so successful in the disguise that the audience didn't realize that it was me playing the role. The atmosphere on the set was excellent. The company was extremely congenial, and the security of being involved in a successful series created an easygoing chemistry in the work. My character was called "Paris." I often wondered if perhaps that name was chosen for me because of my success in a one-name character called Spock. But there was a difference—Paris was a non-character.

Where there had been a great deal of thought given to the internal life of Mr. Spock, Paris had none at all. This was the design of all the characters on *Mission: Impossible*. There was no investigation of who the characters were or their personal interaction with each other. The emphasis was on what they did, what part they played in fulfilling the complex activities of the *Mission* team.

For me the workload was much lighter than it had been on *Star Trek*. In the adventures of the *Enterprise* and its crew, Captain Kirk and Mr. Spock were involved in almost every piece of action that took place. This meant that at least Bill Shatner and I, and quite frequently DeForest Kelley, were required to be on the set and at work most of the twelve-hour shooting day—five days a week. In the case of *M:I* the nature of the script construction gave everybody an occasional work break. We were all gathered for the beginning of the new show when "Phelps" would hand out and explain the assignment, and usually for the last scene of the show when the IMF would gather to drive off, having accomplished the mission. In between, each of the characters would go their own separate ways, most of the time. That being the case, it meant that I wouldn't be required to be on hand when Greg Morris was tunneling through the walls of a building to implant his electronic devices. This kind of dispersion of the workload meant that each of us could have some time, a free day, or certainly in many cases, several free hours of time to relax, study and, in general, conserve some energies.

One thing was very seriously lacking for me. In the time

that I spent on *M:I* I never was emotionally or spiritually
involved with the scripts, as I had been on *Star Trek*. Frankly,
in many cases I didn't even understand them. But this was a
successful show and I thought that perhaps the complications
of the script were part of the success of the series. Somehow
the audience was tantalized by bits of information, believing
that if they watched the set intensely and carefully they would
eventually understand everything that was going on. In retrospect I realized that this was not necessarily the case. In
some instances, the complications of the story were complications for their own sake and really didn't add up in a way that a
perfect jigsaw puzzle would after all the pieces were in place.
In any case I did my work more or less in isolation. I tried to at
least have an understanding of what my scenes were about
and to play them as cameo pieces. All of this was fun for
awhile but eventually I realized that I had done it. I had
played the South American dictator, I had played the Greek
shipping magnate, I had played the European re-
volutionaries. Having done that, and without the sustenance
of personal involvement in the material, the fun began to wear
thin. In the middle of the second season I told my agent that I
would like to ask for a release from the series.

If there is *one* thing that agents dream about in my
business it would be to set each of their actors in a television
series. This would mean that there would be the greatest
potential of possible income and the least amount of effort on
the agent's part. A series means steady work in a business that
offers very little of that phenomenon. And here was the
bizarre and shocking phenomenon of an actor asking to be
unemployed!

It took several weeks before my agent took me seriously.
He assumed that I had had some bad experience on the set or
with the front office at Paramount and in a fit of pique was
asking to get off the series. He did a very good job of waiting
me out before he would take any specific action. I assured him
week after week that there was nothing of the sort in my
motivation. I really meant it when I said that I was getting

bored and that I felt that I was back to simply "working for a living." As a matter of fact it was a very nice living. The next two years of my contract, if I were to fulfill them, would mean a gross of close to three-quarters of a million dollars including residuals. An agent gets ten percent of that. That meant I was asking my agent to give up close to seventy-five thousand dollars in potential income over the next two years. That's a very painful thing for an agent to do.

I had great peace of mind in the decision. I had done extremely well financially in three years of *Star Trek* and two years of *M:I*. I was very anxious to get out and explore other possibilities. Eventually, my agent realized that I was quite serious about my intentions. He went to the studio and after several discussions, a couple of which I joined, we agreed to part amicably and I said goodbye at the end of my second season on the show. I have never regretted that decision.

M:I moved along very nicely without me for another three years until it eventually had run its course and was cancelled. Had I stayed on the show for at least the two additional years of my contract, and possibly the third year to the end of the series, I would have repeated myself professionally and made an awful lot of money. The difference would be that instead of being a rich man today I guess I would have been a *very* rich man today.

The Goodies Box

While being interviewed by Dick Cavett, Katherine Hepburn said: "You come into town with your box of goodies and that box of goodies is you, and you start to use it and sell it and eventually the box of goodies gets used up and then you must go back to something else to fill up the box with some new goodies."

During the two years that followed my departure from *Mission: Impossible* I was able to explore new boundaries in my acting which led to some fantastic theatrical experiences. I was also able to explore photography and writing, which have opened my life immeasurably. I was refilling my "box of goodies." I'm convinced that none of this would have happened if I had comfortably gone on "earning a living" in the security of *Mission: Impossible*.

Most people are so busy doing what they must do that they never have the opportunity to find out what they can do.

For me it was a very exciting time. When I finished working on the *Mission* series, I simply went home and sat down to contemplate. There was enough money in the bank and enough residual income for the future to take care of my family's needs for some time to come. Certainly, I felt secure for at least a year or two if I didn't earn a dime. This, in spite of the fact that our standard of living had crept up to where we were living a very comfortable life in a very large home.

I simply puttered around the house for three or four weeks. I got out in the backyard and I got my hands into the earth, which was something I hadn't the time to do for the last five years. Somewhere inside me there is a reservoir of ideas and creative energy. The last five years of working on series had depleted that reservoir until I could almost see the gauge sitting close to the big "E" mark for Empty. I sensed that I needed some time to absorb, to get back in touch with myself and my family, and the world. I started listening to more music, going to concerts, and theatre, and in general replenishing myself for what I sensed would be the next major movement in my life and career.

My parents' scrapbooks are filled with 2¼ × 3¼ black-and-white photographs of my childhood years. These pictures were shot with a Kodak camera which was popular during the 1930s. It was called a Kodak Autographic and was a very simple lightweight bellows camera which was designed to allow an inscription to be written on the back of the film. That camera fascinated me and became an important part of my life. In my pre-adolescent years I discovered that it was possible to buy small quantities of chemical and paper and to lock myself into the family bathroom with some of our old negatives and turn out black and white prints. There was a magic about it which still fascinates me to this day. To take a sensitized piece of paper and place it next to a negative, expose it to some light and immerse that paper into a tray of developer is still one of the most magical experiences that I can think of.

Throughout my childhood I experimented with it and even built a homemade enlarger from a plan which I discovered in *Mechanics Illustrated* magazine. The bellows camera was the central part of the project and the cost of the additional supplies and equipment must have come to a grand total of around three or four dollars. It included a bread board base, a couple of pieces of lumber for a post, and a metal lunch box for the light housing. When I was around 15 this crude piece of equipment sent me into the business of photographing children in the various neighborhoods around Boston. I would carry the camera, one light and a window blind for a background. I knocked on doors in apartment neighborhoods, offering to photograph children and provide three or four proofs and an 8 × 10 enlargement of their choice for a total of a dollar. After I shot the pictures, I would hurry home to work with my crude equipment in the family bathroom. I really didn't think of it in terms of making money. It was really providing me with an opportunity to use the camera and to spend some time in the magic of that darkroom isolation.

Photography touched my life periodically throughout the years, but in January of 1971 it erupted into a fever. With the encouragement and guidance of Joby Baker, an actor friend of mine and an excellent photographer, I bought my first sophisticated camera. It was a 2¼ format Mamiya 330, a very well-built camera with the advantage of interchangeable lenses. I spent the first few weeks of 1971 shooting everything in sight and rushing into a small room in my house which I had converted into a darkroom to process the product. I was using a very old enlarger that I had bought some years ago at Sears for approximately $30.00 and the results showed it. My work was suffering from bad equipment so I replaced the enlarger with a new piece of equipment. And then I came up against a big question. Why was I shooting pictures?

Since I really didn't have the answer to that question I really didn't know what I wanted to shoot. I knew what I liked when I looked at other photographers' work. I was attracted to nature studies and abstract ideas expressed in black and white photography. The end product intrigued me, but I had no idea what the artist was thinking about in conceiving the images. I felt empty in this area and decided I needed some help.

I enrolled in an extension photography course at UCLA for a series of seven weekly meetings on Thursday evenings. The course stressed vision rather than technique. At this point my condition was very similar to when I started to take acting classes after ten years of working in films and television. I was fairly proficient in technique but I was lacking in motivation and concept. Now I had the time, the technique and with the concepts being awakened in my head I tore into the work with a tremendous sense of new-found worlds to conquer. I spent hours during the day shooting and hours during the night in the darkroom learning to become a proficient printer.

There was a phone in my darkroom and the one thing that I resented most was that phone bell ringing while I was in the midst of creating a visual idea. For many years before *Star Trek* the phone was a central part of our family life. It was the instrument through which I received glad tidings from agents. Now it almost seemed as if an offer of a job would intrude on the most exciting thing that had happened to me in a long time.

The quality of my black-and-white product improved very quickly. I even considered the possibility of finding ways to support a family in this exciting profession. But above all there was a great therapy involved. I was refilling myself and resensitizing myself through a new creative process. And one element stood out first and foremost as being the most important and gratifying of all. I could conceive an idea, shoot it, process it and hold the finished product in my hand. Whatever I did was mine, and I could do it when and how I pleased.

My camera equipment became a part of my baggage wherever I travelled. One day in the darkroom with the red light to work by I fumbled to answer the ringing telephone. There was a print in the developer and my concentration was divided between it and the conversation which followed. The call was from an old friend and motion-picture producer named Euan Lloyd. It was an offer to go to Spain to work in a Western that he was producing starring Yul Brynner and

Richard Crenna. We discussed the possibility briefly, during
which I remember telling him that I had no commitments for
the period of time that he required my services and suggested
that he send a script and get in touch with my agent. I hung
up the phone and went back to what I considered far more
important work which had been interrupted. Somehow it
never occured to me that perhaps I should be excited about
the fact that I was being offered my first motion-picture role in
perhaps eight or ten years.

The picture offered several inducements. It meant an
opportunity to work with some good people. The director was
Sam Wanamaker, an actor and a director whose work I had
always respected in the past. Euan Lloyd and his wife,
Patricia, had been good friends of ours for many years and we
could spend some time with them in Spain, and my old acting
teacher and partner, Jeff Corey, was to appear in the film,
which meant that we would have some pleasant times together on the Mediterranean. Also, and this was very important, it meant that I could see some new and exciting photographic opportunities. As carefully as I packed my clothing I
put together my camera equipment and some developing
supplies so that I could at least process my own film, and
together with my family I prepared for the trip.

At this point in time I had grown a fairly well-developed
beard. It had started as a kick, but had become acceptable
when Sam Wanamaker commented that it would be useful for
the role that I was to play in the western. I was due to leave
for Spain on April 7th, to be followed by my family approximately a week later.

During the last week in March I made a trip to New York
which was eventually to take me to Boston for a visit with my
family. The New York trip was a political favor. I was to make
an appearance at a fund-raiser for a lady running for Congress.
I found myself with some free time one day while staying at
the Warwick Hotel in mid-Manhattan.

Eric Schepard, a theatrical agent at International Famous
Agency in New York, had been, as a matter of record, my
theatrical representative for the past three or four years. We

had never actually investigated or concluded any activities since I had been so totally unavailable because of my commitments. Now it seemed as though it might make sense to at least have our first face-to-face meeting to talk about possibilities for the future.

I called Eric and told him that I was across the street at the Warwick and had some open time. He invited me to come over and visit, which I did. We talked for a few minutes about various possibilities for the future. Eric is an imaginative agent. I guess it was the beard that got to him that day because he asked if I would be interested in playing Tevye in *Fiddler on the Roof*. I told him that I certainly would and he made a phone call to Stephen Slane, producer of the North Shore Music Theatre in Beverly, Massachusetts. Slane was, with his director, Ben Shaktman, in the process of casting a production to take place that summer. I met Slane and Shaktman about an hour later and did a very clumsy audition for them—I was totally unprepared and knew only what I had heard in the way of music for the show and had only a slim idea of the story line. I had never seen a production of *Fiddler on the Roof*. Slane, Shaktman and I spent a couple of hours together exploring the possibilities and discussing my schedule. *Fiddler* would go into rehearsal almost immediately after I was scheduled to finish my picture work in Spain. Shaktman was hesitant. He felt that to do the job properly the actor playing Tevye should be available in New York before actual rehearsals started to at least discuss and explore other dimensions of the role and to give it proper preparation. We set another meeting for the next morning and that night I went to see *Fiddler on the Roof* on Broadway.

To me it was an overwhelming experience. Not because the production was that good. It wasn't. *Fiddler* at that point had been running for approximately eight years and I'm sorry to say that what I saw on stage did not reach the full potential of the material. However, I was thrilled with the possibility of playing the role. I completely identified with the characters on stage. Their story was the story of my own family and their experience in an eventual emigration from Russia.

In the morning I felt fully armed and prepared to convince Slane and Shaktman that I now knew exactly what the piece was all about and how I would approach it and what I could bring to it as an actor. At the appointed time of the meeting, 9:15 A.M., the phone in my hotel rang. I assumed that this meant Slane and Shaktman had arrived for our meeting. On the contrary, it was Mr. Slane calling me to tell me that they were not coming because Mr. Shaktman felt that the possibility of doing the job properly was too slim because of my schedule. I could see a great and exciting opportunity slipping away and decided that I had to grasp it before it was gone. I asked Slane if I might contact and talk with Shaktman personally. He assured me that he would be delighted if I would do that. He felt that I could do the role but it was the director, Shaktman, who had reservations. I called Shaktman and poured out my story on the phone. I told him about my own background and the background of my family and my very personal and deep identification with the characters of the play. Somehow I even managed to throw in a reference to Bertolt Brecht's *Mother Courage*. The concept of the man, the family and the wagon somehow were analogous to Brecht's heroine. It was a lucky stroke. Shaktman had directed a production of *Mother Courage* in Europe and my comments touched a responsive chord. He asked if we could meet at the musical conductor's apartment within the next hour.

An hour later I walked into the apartment of Herb Grossman on Park Avenue in New York. Herb was to be the conductor for the tour. I had never met a more gifted, sensitive and giving individual in my theatrical experiences. I found myself in the company of two men whose ideas and energy and attitudes and talent moved me and excited me very deeply. Something in that meeting, the chemistry, the timing, the people, the project involved, brought out the best in me and I gave a very successful audition. Shaktman admitted that he was shaken. I think that he had gone through the motions of the meeting simply as a kindness in response to the onslaught of my enthusiasm. Now he was really in a position where he had to re-evaluate all of his thinking about the casting of the famous milkman, Tevye. A tall, skinny Tevye who was best known for having played a character with pointed ears was not quite what he had in mind when he first started thinking about the role. He told me that he'd give it serious consideration, asked where he could reach me during the next few days and we parted very warmly. At the least, I felt that I had given it my best shot.

I went to Boston and spent a day with my parents and then returned to California to prepare for the trip to Spain.

I was back in Los Angeles on Thursday evening, April 1st, and spent a long three days wondering about Shaktman's thoughts about our working together. The following Wednesday, I was scheduled to leave for Spain. On Monday morning I had run out of patience. I could no longer be cool and wait for a phone call. I called Eric Schepard to tell him that I had to make some decisions. Either I was to leave immediately for New York to spend some time with Shaktman and Grossman, or else the opportunity would be lost and I would be off to Spain without the *Fiddler* script.

While I had Eric Schepard on the phone and was putting the questions to him, he was receiving a call from Ben Shaktman, who was trying to reach me. Schepard said, "Hang up—Ben Shaktman will be calling you momentarily." I did as I was told, answered the phone when it rang, and heard Ben Shaktman say, "Are you still interested in playing Tevye?" The next morning I was on my way to New York. I spent much of the next 24 hours working with Shaktman and Grossman in a small studio with a piano. On a cassette recorder we taped all of the music that I could work on while I was away. We parted with much excitement and much anticipation. I left for Spain with *Fiddler on the Roof, Catlow,* which was the western I was about to do, and my camera all neatly tucked away in my baggage.

Within 90 days of having completed my work on *Mission: Impossible* I had stepped onto a platform which would rocket me off in three major areas. A motion picture, a very exciting theatrical tour and a photographic trip.

Live Long and Prosper—L'Chaim

There are times when all the elements in my life seem to come together and make sense in one grand design. At those times I feel I know exactly what I am doing and why I am doing it. With apologies to Abraham Lincoln there are also times when I know what I am doing but don't know why I am doing it, or, I am not sure what I am doing but think I know why.

I had commited myself to a seven-week trip to Spain to appear in a Western. The part was very small in spite of the fact that I was to receive star billing above the title with Yul Brynner and Richard Crenna. But I instinctively felt that I was not there for the sake of making the movie. I hope my good friend and producer, Euan Lloyd, will understand when I say that I had ulterior motives. I was there to work with Sam Wanamaker, to prepare for *Fiddler on the Roof,* and to shoot pictures.

Sam turned out to be every bit as creative as I had hoped. He had a very extensive and impressive theatrical background, including a lot of Shakespeare. He had played Iago to Paul Robeson's Othello, and was at that time beginning to make plans for a new Shakespearean theatre in England. I told Sam that I was interested in getting into theatrical activity, including the classics. He told me that the Globe Theatre in San Diego would be very interested in having me appear and urged me to contact them. The Globe Theatre has for many years had a very fine reputation for its production of Summer Shakespearean Festivals. I sent them a letter expressing my interest and made a tentative appointment to see them upon my return from Spain. The meeting did eventually take place and paid off with unexpected dividends.

Since my role in *Catlow* was small, I had a lot of free time. Much of it was spent wandering around the hillsides of Costa del Sol shooting pictures of everything in sight. Then I would head back to my hotel room where I would lock myself into the bathroom, as I had when I was a child, and process my film.

When I wasn't shooting pictures or tracking Yul Brynner I would spend my time lying on the Mediterranean beaches listening to my tape tracks of music to *Fiddler on the Roof.* I'm sure I was a strange and exotic sight for the Spanish locals. Mr. Spock on the beach in a bathing suit and beard listening to Semitic songs on a cassette recorder!

There was very little television available in the remote towns on the southern coast of Spain at that time. This meant that I was free to roam around the streets of the villages as would any English or American sightseer. *Star Trek* did manage to catch up with me in a surprising way. Around the second week of shooting I was sitting in the make-up chair in the portable trailer which was used for the make-up department on the *Catlow* production. The make-up man was a friendly young man from Madrid who spoke fairly good English and let me practice my bad Spanish on him. On this particular day there was a gleam in his eye when he said, "I have something to show you." He reached down inside his cabinet and pulled out a small wooden cigar box.

You can imagine my shock when he reached in and pulled out a pair of my foam-rubber pointed ears. I was really amazed. Not only did I not expect him to be aware of *Star Trek* and Mr. Spock but, to see a pair of my ears left me dumbfounded. The explanation was simple. The ear pieces for *Star Trek* had been made by a master make-up man named John Chambers. Mr. Chambers specialized in "appliances," which are the very delicate foam rubber pieces used to change an actor's appearance. He later won an Academy Award for his work on *Planet of the Apes*. Chambers had been in Spain working on a picture and my make-up man had worked for him as an assistant. During that time Chambers, being a generous man with his talents, had spent some time with the Spanish make-up artists instructing them in the use of appliances. He had brought some samples of his work from the States, including several pair of the Spock ears. These he distributed to some of the make-up men in Spain, and that's how my ears ended up in a cigar box in Almeria.

Later that year, on a visit to London, I was a guest at the home of the Paramount sales representative. His son was a very nice young man in his teens. The conversation eventually turned to *Star Trek* and his father suggested that he go to the closet in the hall. This he did and, to my surprise, came back with a complete Mr. Spock uniform. The blue shirt, the black trousers and the black boots. They looked exactly like mine. The fact of the matter is that they were mine! The father was a very enterprising gentleman and because his son's interest in *Star Trek* was so intense he had contacted Paramount in Hollywood after production of the show had finished. I was amazed to discover that he had actually been able to persuade someone at Paramount wardrobe to send him a complete Mr. Spock uniform.

Somehow it gave me a feeling that pieces of me had been scattered all over the world. To this day all that I own as a physical reminder of *Star Trek* is a lot of photographs and one pair of pointed ears, which my wife, Sandi, had mounted in a plastic box which sits on the fireplace mantle in my den.

After three or four weeks of shooting on *Catlow* I had a break in the schedule which allowed me to take four or five days off. I took advantage of this opportunity to fly to London to take care of some business. While there I spent an evening in the theatre in the West End watching the London production of *Fiddler on the Roof*. In this case, as in New York, the production was somewhat tired and tacky since it had been running for approximately four to five years. However, my own concepts about the material were reaffirmed and I felt even more confident about my future in the role.

On June 10th, my work in *Catlow* was completed and I returned to Los Angeles. Three days later I arrived in San Diego for my first meeting with Craig Noel and Adrienne Butler at the Old Globe Theatre. We had a lengthy and stimulating conversation about mutual interests in the theatre. However, there was a problem. The Globe Theatre operates in repertory, which means that an actor must commit to a minimum of two and a half to three months of work and as much as four months to work the summer season. One would work in more than one production and would do the plays in repertory throughout the summer. This was far more time than I had planned to commit myself and, in any case, that summer was out of the question since I was already scheduled to do *Fiddler on the Roof*.

They pointed out to me that they had a winter season which was a possibility and suggested that they submit to me a list of plays which they would produce if there were one that I felt strongly enough about doing later that year. They sent me the list which included *The Man In The Glass Booth*. That was the play I chose, and it was decided that it would be the opening play of their fall season which I would do when I finished with my *Fiddler* tour.

Ten days after my San Diego meeting I was back in New York on June 24th to begin active preparation for our production of *Fiddler*.

From the day the work began it was obvious that this was
going to be one of those situations where I knew exactly what
I was doing and why I was doing it. The company that
Stephen Slane and Ben Shaktman had assembled was absolutely first rate. The rehearsals went beautifully and Shaktman proved to be an extraordinary director. With his inven-
tive and sensitive guidance and the incredible musical support of Herb Grossman, a family of twenty-five people came
together in what for me was one of the greatest experiences of
my life.

We rehearsed in New York and then the company moved
to Hyannis, Massachusetts, where we were to play the first
two weeks of a seven-week tour.

On the first evening that I spent in Hyannis, I walked over
to take a look at the theatre with Ben Shaktman. The theatre
there consists of a multicolored canvas tent in the round with
a very deep rake down to a stage which almost seems to be in
a pit. By this time our *Fiddler* troupe had become a very
Jewish company, and I found it very ironic that the performance given that night was the *Sound of Music*. As Ben and I
watched the performance from the top of one of the aisles I
turned to him and said, "This week the Christians are in the
pit, next week they'll throw in the Jews."

Fiddler on the Roof at that time was an event. It was the
first time that the show had been released for production in
stock theatres around the country. Our performances were
widely anticipated and sold out in advance. Opening night
was full of excitement for me particularly because I was
playing in my home state of Massachusetts. And many of my
family and friends were in the opening night audience.

This was my first time on stage in front of a theatre
audience in over three years. My last appearance had been in
a light farce called *Visit to a Small Planet* in a dinner theatre in
Illinois. There was no comparison. Opening night was indicative of things to come. We played to an audience tingling with
anticipation. The company was high-spirited, well-rehearsed
and "up" for an exciting evening. Even the thunderous storm

which temporarily halted the show couldn't dampen the spirits of that night.

The show played beautifully, filled with laughter and tears. When it was over we all knew what we had done and why we had done it. A packed house of 1,600 people were on their feet giving us a standing ovation and acting as if they didn't want to leave the theatre. It was the beginning of seven precious and glorious weeks in the life of a man with pointed ears.

Elliot Norton, the respected drama critic from Boston, came to see the show. He referred to us as the "pleasant surprise of the summer season." It was no surprise to us. We knew who we were, what we were doing and why.

We played to capacity houses, extra performances and standing ovations in Hyannis and Beverly, Massachusetts; Rochester, New York; and Toledo, Ohio. Six weeks later we were back for a return and closing engagement in Hyannis. They had been weeks of exquisite beauty. The condition where one knows that all is right and a very special event is taking place in one's life, where everyday regardless of the weather, the city, the food, the hotel room, is a special day. It was like the best of *Star Trek*. When one walks with pride and with a special spring in the walk because the vehicle, the company, the time have all come together in some kind of special magic confluence to create a mystic aura which stops time in its tracks and will become an unforgettable memory to be relived again and again.

We had rented a beach house at Hyannis and I was driving from the house to the theatre for an evening performance in the final week of the run. I was humming songs from the show when I was caught by a flood of emotion and heard myself say, "If I never act again it will be okay." That was saying a lot. It was saying that I had had the opportunity to act in a great vehicle, under great direction, both dramatic and musical, and with a great company of talent—singers, actors and dancers. I was riding on the crest of a wave and I knew it. When a good thing is happening in one's life that is something special. When a good thing is happening in someone's life and he knows it—that's a miracle. I was involved in a miracle and I knew that I could always look back on it with a sense of good fortune. "If I never act again, it will be okay." I had been there. I had had it all. I could never again feel frustrated or deprived.

I arrived at the theatre about an hour before curtain time. For the next half hour I would work out at a piano with Sean Daniels, who was playing the Constable in the show and was an excellent vocal coach. Sean and I were in the habit of warming up my voice for approximately twenty minutes, after which we would each go to our dressing rooms to prepare for the performance. During my warm-up I noticed a few members of the cast drifting into the rehearsal hall we were using. Gradually more and more of the company members drifted in and I became somewhat self-conscious and aware that something unusual was taking place.

Before I knew it the entire company had assembled and were surrounding Sean and me at the piano. They apologized and stopped my warm-up. Then one of the company stepped forward and said, "We have something we want to give you." They handed me a ribbon-wrapped box. I opened it and discovered a pair of gorgeous pewter candelabras. It was a gift to Sandi and me from the company and on the base of the candelabras they had had inscribed a phrase from the Sabbath prayer song in *Fiddler on the Roof* . The phrase said, "Favor them Oh Lord with happiness and peace." I held the candlesticks in my hand and tried to tell them of my thoughts driving to the performance that evening. I said, "Your timing is incredible. You don't know what this means to me. Driving to the theatre this evening in my car, I was saying to myself, if I never act again . . ." and that's as far as I got. I was in tears and could speak no more. For the next few minutes, twenty-five of the most beautiful singers, actors and dancers that it will ever be my privilege to work with, were huddled in tearful joy. That night's audience who watched the performance of *Fiddler on the Roof* were treated to a holy communion of the human spirit.

I believe there is a danger in the concept that "opportunity knocks." Taken literally this might mean that all one needs to do is to sit and listen for the sound of knuckles on wood. My feeling is quite the contrary and always has been. I believe that it's through the individual's commitment to various ideas and projects that one discovers surprising opportunities. At least that's the way it's always worked for me. I don't believe that there is such a thing as "waste of time" involved when a person is pursuing an idea, a project, a hobby, a social cause, or whatever motivates him.

I was in New York for a political cause when I first met Eric Schepard, the agent at International Famous Agency who introduced me to the summer musical theatre possibilities which led to my appearing in *Fiddler on the Roof* and other musicals such as *Oliver, The King and I,* and *Camelot.*

It was my decision to go to Spain to appear in a rather slim role in *Catlow* which led to working with Sam Wanamaker which led to a discussion about the Old Globe Theatre which led to a very enriching production of *The Man in the Glass Booth.*

During the course of an unrewarding stay at Universal Studios in 1972 I spent much of the time shooting and processing a lot of black and white prints. I had quite a collection of material when one day my wife, Sandi, arrived home with a book in hand. It was called *Love Is An Attitude* by Walter Rinder. It had attracted her attention in a bookstore, because it consisted of photographs and poetry. Sandi felt that it might be a format that I could use, since much of my photography lent itself to this kind of material. These are the times when one is grateful for an efficient assistant/secretary. Teresa Victor had zealously guarded and filed every poem, phrase or thought that I had scribbled in my travels. We pulled out the files and went to work putting together words and pictures.

It wasn't too long before a potential idea for a book began to emerge. Some of the pictures lent themselves to verbal ideas and some of the notes or thoughts I had gathered suggested photographic images. I went to work on both. Then

I contacted Celestial Arts in San Francisco who were the publishers of the Rinder book. They agreed to print the work under the title, *You and I*. I was about to become a published author.

As an actor I discovered that I really was hiding behind characters—nobody knew who I really was. I'm saying somebody else's words and, in the most public profession of all, retaining my own privacy. Hiding identity behind characters. "Maybe I'm saying words and ideas that agree with my own but they are not mine, they didn't spring from me—I'm interpreting somebody else's ideas even if I do relate to them personally." And getting into writing is suddenly a very dangerous and scary experience because it is personal and it is real. It is a naked experience. It's like saying, "Okay, judge me, this is really me." If you don't like the character that I play then I can really hide behind that and say, "Well, that's not really me, you can dislike the character but don't blame me."

I had a fantasy of trying to publish material in a private way by going to a very small publishing company and figuring that they would only print a few thousand copies; maybe I could buy most of them myself and give them away to relatives and friends. But then a quarter of a million copies were printed and the book was no longer private.

Then the feedback started. Very lovely feedback coming from people who are touched by the material and say, "Yes, I feel that way, too." And you start to realize that it's okay to be out there and be honest and open about yourself because you are part of the human race and other people respond the same way and have had the same feelings and are touched by it and that gives you courage to write some more and say some more personal things. In 1974 Celestial Arts published my second books of poems and photographs entitled *Will I Think of You?* These books have added another rich dimension to my life.

This is a career built on *Star Trek* . . . I can feel the influences all around me. The unique aspects of the Vulcan character have attracted a lot of press attention as well as offers to appear in motion pictures and television shows.

Much of the material that I am offered to do in films is pretty bad. It consists of bad science fiction, or bad horror films, for the most part. But there is nothing to complain about. Obviously, I can keep busy doing projects that are very exciting.

There are always those first few moments of my appearance in the theatre when people look for the Spock character and make an adjustment to Leonard Nimoy in this particular role. We get past that quickly and I never find it to be a very serious problem.

There is an occasional exception. Once during a performance in the theatre-in-the-round I was moving slowly down a darkened aisle waiting to make an entrance on stage. I was deeply involved in my character and that evening's performance when I was startled by a little voice coming from one of the seats nearby. He whispered quietly, "Hi, Mr. Spock."